Sport, Culture, Politics
and Scottish Society

Irish Immigrants and the
Gaelic Athletic Association

J6

)07

Dedicated to those who perished as a consequence
of the Great Famine in Ireland 1845–49

Sport, Culture, Politics and Scottish Society

Irish Immigrants and the Gaelic Athletic Association

JOSEPH M BRADLEY

JOHN DONALD PUBLISHERS LTD
EDINBURGH

ISBN 0 85976 481 8

British Library Cataloguing in Publication Data.
A catalogue record for this book is available
from the British Library.

Bank of Ireland

The author would like to acknowledge
the financial assistance of the Bank of
Ireland in relation to the research which
has made this book possible

Typesetting & prepress origination by Brinnoven, Livingston.
Printed & bound in Great Britain by Bell & Bain Ltd, Glasgow.

CONTENTS

Joe Mc Donagh
President of the G.A.A.

FOREWORD

Teachtaireacht ó Uachtarán Chumann Lúthchleas Gael

Fearaim fíor-chaoin fáilte roimh an bhfoilseachán suimiúil spreagúil seo faoi stair Chumann Lúthchleas Gael in Albain. Tréaslaím a shaothar leis an údar, An Seosamh Ó Brolcháin, agus gabhaim buíochas ó chroí leis as ucht an leabhar tábhachtach seo a chur ar fáil dúinn.

In welcoming this publication from Joseph Bradley, as President of the Gaelic Athletic Association, I wish to thank him sincerely for providing us with a valuable insight into the history of our Association in Scotland. Indeed, the fortunes of the G.A.A. in Scotland, since the first club was founded in 1897 (Red Hugh O Neills of Glasgow), are very much linked to the fortunes of the Irish who emigrated to Scotland. The organisation has experienced highs and lows over the past one hundred years but it has always fought back to regain a place in the consciousness of Irish identity amongst the Irish community in Scotland.

I wish to pay a particular tribute to those men and women who have struggled to sustain the Association and its sports through all of those difficult times. It was not an easy task and unfortunately their efforts in the early days were never fully appreciated by our own leaders back home. Of course, they had their own struggles in Ireland, to develop and nurture the fledgling organisation into the strong Association it is today. Thankfully, those attitudes have now all changed. Through the efforts of the International Dimension Committees of the past ten years, our members in Ireland have a greater appreciation of what our overseas units have achieved for our emigrants and diaspora abroad.

Just as the celebration of the Centenary of 1984 helped to focus the Gaels of Scotland on a revival of Gaelic games and sports there, similarly, I believe that Dr Bradley's work will also concentrate minds yet again on the wonderful and exciting possibilities of the future for the G.A.A. in Scotland. It is indeed a fitting tribute to all who have striven to create an identity, through the medium of our Gaelic games, for our Irish kindred in Scotland. May it inspire many others, both emigrants and those of Irish descent, to enhance the wonderful tradition of our games in Scotland which have enjoyed a renaissance in recent times.

Finally, I wish to thank the Bank of Ireland for their generous assistance towards the research for this important work. Their support indicates a deep appreciation of what the author has undertaken on behalf of the Association in Scotland. Indeed, he has unveiled for us all a greater understanding of ourselves as a people.

Fada go maire cine Gael na hAlban dílis dár gcluichí Gaelacha. Guím gach rath ar an leabhar breá seo agus go dtuga Dia an luach saothair atá tuillte aige don údar féin.

Seosamh Mac Donncha (Joseph McDonagh)
Uachtarán C.L.G. (President, G.A.A.)

LIST OF TABLES

LIST OF ILLUSTRATIONS

24. Paisley Gaels, 1996.
25. Scotland County Squad 'Irish International Football Tournament', Dublin, 1996.
26. Tir Conail Harps, Glasgow, 1997.
27. Shotts Gaels, 1997.
28. Shotts Gaels, Camogie, 1997.
29. Charlie Quinn and John Keaveney at the newly-purchased Eastfield Park in Glasgow, 1953.
30. Cois Tine, Glasgow, marking the Feast of St Brigid, 1978.
31. Pearse Memorial Cross, Pearse Park.
32. Early Efforts to re-start hurling and Camogie in Glasgow, 1988.
33. Programme for the Strathclyde Irish Festival, 1989.
34. Glasgow's Lord Provost, Susan Baird, with Owen McAuley, a local Irish dancer, launching the 1990 Strathclyde Irish Festival during Glasgow's European reign as the City of Culture.
35. President of Ireland, Mary Robinson, is welcomed by local politicians on her visit to representatives of Glasgow's Irish organisations in 1992.
36. Members of Sands MacSwiney's G.F.C. welcome the 1993 All-Ireland Football winning coach, Mickey Moran, of Derry, and the Sam Maguire trophy to Coatbridge.
37. T P Murphy (International Workgroup) and G.A.A. President, Jack Bootham, at St Jude's Primary School, Barlanark, Glasgow, for the launch of the Coaching Pilot Scheme, 1994.
38. Celtic Football Club. The primary focus and manifestation of 'Irishness' amongst the Irish dispora in Scotland.
39. Jimmy McHugh, Anne Doherty, Anne McHugh and Owen Kelly, founding members in the 1950s of the Irish Minstrels' Branch of Comhaltas Ceoltoiri Eireann, the first branch to be founded in Britain.
40. Tir Conail Harps v. Lochgilphead, shinty/camogie, 1996.
41. Paddy Gavigan, of Mulroy Gaels, receives the football championship trophy on the centenary of the founding of the first G.A.A. club in Glasgow. Molly Quinn and Owen Kelly make the presentation at Pearse Park in September, 1997.

INTRODUCTION

In recent years sport has become a topic for the study of society as well as a variety of social, cultural and political features of individuals, groups, communities and nations. Using the focus of Ireland's gaelic sporting traditions, the aim of this work is to advance the study of the Irish abroad: in particular, to study aspects of the Scottish element of the Irish diaspora.

For many reading about the Gaelic Athletic Association (G.A.A.), and for others reading of aspects of the Irish immigrant experience, this book will serve as an introduction to a growing area of research. It also adds to the exploration of various aspects of Irish identity, especially amongst the Irish abroad. This work celebrates the centenary of the founding of the first gaelic club, Red Hugh O Neills, amongst the Irish immigrant community in Glasgow in 1897. As a study of a sporting expression or variant, in looking at the Gaelic Athletic Association this work is not concerned with a history of exercise, movement or the many other aesthetic or commercial aspects of sport. Rather, this investigation embraces elements of a sociological, historical and political nature. Most importantly, sport is viewed as an appropriate avenue for illuminating the Irish experience in Scotland.[1]

Conquest, colonisation and the resultant conflict in Ireland's history, has meant that culture and identity amongst the Irish has long been characterised by questions of a broadly political nature. For this reason, and particularly because of the roots and history of the Gaelic Athletic Association, politics has an important contribution in any account of the G.A.A. as well as of the Irish diaspora in general. In an effort to understand some of the cultural and political beliefs and attitudes as well as the frame of reference which inhabits the Irish perspective it is also important to enter the Irish mind-set. Historically, of course, there has been a vast number of perspectives and mind-sets in Ireland, but the notion remains that dominant cultural and political ideas and views amongst the Irish have frequently been critically different from Scottish and British ones generally, and these have broadly to be engaged if an understanding of the Irish, the Irish diaspora and the G.A.A. in Britain is to be developed. For these reasons this book explores some Irish perspectives on the historical conflict as well as tensions that have existed between Ireland and Britain. Overall therefore, this book examines some of the social, cultural and political perspectives of the Irish in Ireland and Scotland.

The initial parts of this work look at the significance of sport in the general cultural and political arenas. Subsequently, it reflects on the origins, importance and character of the Gaelic Athletic Association in both Ireland and Scotland. Against this background of Irish and Scottish historical development, the book examines the location and participants in gaelic games in Scotland as well as registering who was present and who achieved what in sporting, cultural and political contexts. This has as much to do with recording aspects of familial histories as it has with gaining further insight into the individuals and communities involved. A drawing together of a number of strands also enables further research into the Irish in Scotland.

The latter sections of the book will analyse the Gaelic Athletic Association, specifically with a view to gaining more insight into ideas of Irishness and Irish identity in modern Scotland. In terms of these identities, particular reference is made to the effects of conflict in Northern Ireland as this has made a significant impact upon questions of modern Irishness within Ireland as well as wherever the Irish have settled. However, this book is not an exploration of Irish identity, although the nature and function of Irishness amongst the offspring of Irish immigrants in Scotland does form an important sub-theme of the book. Likewise, although there is much academic debate in relation to terms such as nationality, identity, community, sectarianism, etc, this book is primarily a history of the Gaelic Athletic Association in Scotland, in the context of the G.A.A. among the Irish in Ireland as well as its diaspora. Questions of political and cultural Irishness are raised throughout the book, but this is pursued by way of background and context, and is necessary for a greater understanding of the G.A.A.

Although a fuller insight into the Irish in modern Scotland will follow publication of this commemorative work, and notwithstanding the fact that this research will necessarily entail a more acuminate exploration of the noted terms, this book remains a research exercise which partly fills one of the many gaps in research into the Irish in Scotland.[2] As well as celebrating the G.A.A. in Scotland and Ireland, it is also a contribution to the historical, social and political development of Scotland's largest single immigrant grouping.

Notes

1. See Bradley, 1995.
2. Bradley, forthcoming.

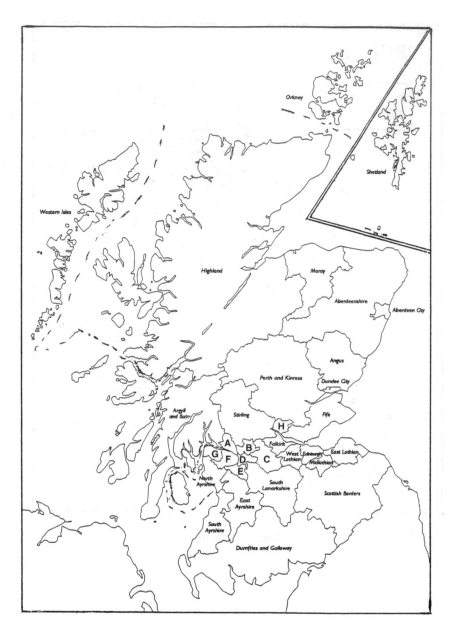

Map 1. Local Authorities, Scotland

Key: A, West Dunbartonshire; B, East Dunbartonshire;
C, North Lanarkshire; D, City of Glasgow; E, East
Renfrewshire; F, Renfrewshire; G, Inverclyde;
H, Clackmannanshire

Map 2. Ireland.

ACKNOWLEDGEMENTS

The help and assistance of the many individuals who supplied information and photographic material, and in other ways contributed to this project, is gratefully acknowledged. In addition, players, managers, officials, past and present, of gaelic clubs in Scotland, by virtue of their involvement in gaelic sports, they have made this work possible. Go raibh maith agaibh.

CHAPTER 1

THE SIGNIFICANCE OF SPORT

For many of them the only link with Ireland is supporting Glasgow Celtic, flying the Tricolour and singing patriotic songs at Celtic Park. Most of them forget about Ireland for the rest of the week.[1]

Identity

The above remark from a commentator on Irish affairs encapsulates some aspects of the discourse which relates to Irish identity in modern Scotland. It reflects on people of Irish antecedents who to some observers, do not appear to use more 'authentic' Irish dimensions in their expressions of emotional attachment, loyalty and allegiance to an Irish heritage and identity. Such commentary also embraces a notion that sport can have a distracting or dysfunctional role in the serious business of life, particularly those aspects which reflect in political and cultural activity. Such a conception has been characteristic of a number of Marxist writers like Miliband and Hobsbawm.[2] Jim Sillars, the former Scottish National Party member of parliament also gave substance to this way of thinking with his comment shortly after the announcement of the results of the 1992 British General Election:

> The great problem is that Scotland has too many ninety minute patriots whose nationalist outpourings are expressed only at major sporting events.[3]

Therefore, for people like Sillars, it is unsatisfactory that many people who profess Scottish identity (typified here in football or rugby support), fail to rise above the mediocrity of expressing their allegiances through the vehicle and passion of sport: thus failing to translate their identities into something more tangible and credible. Nonetheless, also inherent in this argument is a recognition that sport has the potential to be an agent of both social consciousness and political socialisation, and is one that should not be ignored in the social sciences.

Of course, sport has a number of psychological and sociological functions. In both Scotland and Ireland, as well as in other societies, sport has contributed considerably to ideas about identity in particular, images and ideas which inform and concern community, nation and culture. It has also meant that no single notion of identity can explain the social, cultural and political formations and structures which people employ in the context of a variety of circumstances.

Over the course of the past generation, sports history and studies have undergone a major transformation. A growing literature on the links between politics, culture, identity and sport is evidence of the recognition amongst social scientists of the value in researching areas of life which may not at first sight seem any more virtuous than relaxing, wasteful or exhilarating pastimes. Undoubtedly, commentators like Sillars and Miliband have a case that sport has a part to play as a culture of evasion, that is, a substitute for involvement or substantial concern with issues which may be more intrinsically fundamental to the economic, social and political orders. For example, during the period of Communist rule in the former Soviet Union, people were constantly faced with a 'propaganda of success'. Repression and suffering were masked as citizens believed the contrivances of the state machine, where the state's ideology was a substitute for original thinking, an opiate of the people, and where as one Soviet worker explained, 'all we could do was chat over a beer, and we were far more interested in sport'.[4]

Nonetheless, regardless of its often functionally suppressive role in a number of cases, the intensity of feeling and elevated place in which sport is placed in many cultures, societies and countries, is also testament to its ingrained and inherent inability to remain simply, 'sport': as an enterprise viewed and expressed simply as a pastime and form of physical activity and having little value above or beyond its recreational functions. But, as Sugden and Bairner state, sport is 'an important bridge between the individual and society'.[5] Where a particular sport is deemed important, it is unlikely to remain detached and autonomous from the rest of society, including its politics. Indeed, histories of sporting institutions show that without social, communal or political emotion and definition, sport is unlikely to have gained its present status or importance in the modern world.

As one Scottish journalist wrote, at an international level, sport matters:

countless government reports have extolled its virtues in improving the nation's health and fitness, keeping down crime and creating wealth through jobs and tourism. Above all, it adds to a country's international prestige. Success makes its citizens feel good and countries that do not perform well at international level are sick countries.[6]

Such meaning can be replicated throughout societies and communities as well as for individuals, and sport can provide a substantial resource for creating and sustaining a variety of identities. In addition, such identities can and often do link with other identities in society which might be regarded as being more fundamental by those such as the 'evasionist theorists'. Sport can also serve to raise cultural, social and political consciousness.[7]

Considering how much time is given to sport within modern lifestyles, by individuals, communities as well as the media and significant financial institutions, one begins to appreciate the central role which sport has historically played in man's affairs. The origins of the Olympic games and even of the games of hurling in Ireland and shinty in Scotland shows that sport has a long and influential history in many societies. As Hoberman states, sport has no intrinsic value structure, but it is a ready and flexible vehicle through which ideological associations can be reinforced.[8] The importance of symbols has been crucial to people throughout history, and sport has a central role in the manufacture and sustenance of many of the symbols which have significance for groups of people, regardless of size, constituency or identity. The history of the Gaelic Athletic Association, as a history of struggle for the survival and expression of Irish identity, reflects Hoberman's assertion.

For over one hundred years identity in much of Ireland has often been defined with a significant strain of passion for gaelic sports. This passion has invoked nationalist, political, cultural as well as purely sporting sensibilities. For 'gaels' many of these passions came together in gaelic sport with the formation of the Gaelic Athletic Association in 1884. The G.A.A. is an element in the sociology, history, culture and political nature of Ireland. It forms part of the story of the people of Ireland, including its diaspora, and it reflects on activities which run deep in Irish consciousness. Apart from the Catholic Church and the country's political parties, the gaelic sports body assumes a commanding presence in Irish life. In addition, the G.A.A. has seen its influence spread among the Irish in the USA and Britain, and its games have been played in almost every country which has experienced a sizeable Irish presence.

Notes

1. T Main, Irish Post, 15/8/87.
2. See Jarvie and Walker, 1994, p. 1.
3. Jenkins, 1983, p. 3.
4. The Peoples Century, BBC Television, 16/2/97.
5. Sugden and Bairner, 1993, p. 9.
6. J Watson, Scotland on Sunday, 16/2/97, p. 8.
7. See Bradley, 1995.
8. Hoberman, 1984.

1. Archbishop Croke

2. Maurice Davin

3. Michael Cusack

4. *Patrick W Nally*

5. John M'Court. Irish activist from Lanarkshire during the early 20th century. Member of Patrick Sarsfield's Hurling Club, Coatbridge; First President of the Provincial Council of Scotland (G.A.A.); Member of the Ancient Order of Hibernians (A.O.H.); Member of the League of the Cross; Treasurer and Organiser of the Irish National Forresters (Scotland).

CHAPTER 2

GAELIC SPORT: IRELAND AND ITS DISPORA

> The tradition of nationality, which meant not only the urge of the
> people to possess the soil and its products, but the free development
> of spiritual, cultural and imaginative qualities of the race, had been
> maintained not by intellectuals but by the people who were
> themselves, the guardians of the remnants of culture.[1]

Origins and evolution of the G.A.A.

Hurling, the premier game of the Gael, has a history going back
at least two thousand years. The tribes and heroes of ancient
Ireland, the Firbolgs, Tuatha de Danaan, the Red Branch Knights
and Cuchulain, from the famous Irish sagas, have all made their
mark in the evolution of hurling. There was an attempt to ban the
game in the 14th century under the colonial administration's
'Statutes of Kilkenny'. Again in 1527 the 'Statute of Galway'
ordered that no hurling should take place whilst the 1695 Sunday
Observance Act enacted, 'that no person or persons whatsoever,
shall play or exercise any hurling'.[2] Although acts like the Statutes
of Kilkenny and of Galway were meant to dissuade early English
colonists from adopting Irish ways and becoming 'more Irish than
the Irish', in creating these laws the forces of conquest in Ireland
also displayed the intention of subverting Irish pastimes and
identities. Thus, for many centuries, even before the birth of the
Gaelic Athletic Association, sport in Ireland exhibited political
resonances.

By the 18th century it is quite clear that there were two
principal, and regionally distinct, versions of the game. The
northern half of the country played the version called caman,
anglicised as 'commons'. The southern half of the country played
the game known as ioman or baire. The main differences in both
versions was that the latter was played during the Summer with a
soft ball or sliothar which could be handled. The version played
in the Northern part of the country was mainly a Winter game in
which the ball could not be handled.[3] Although the game today is
unrecognisable from its unstructured and often violent

antecedents, of all gaelic sports it is hurling which owes its origins to the gaelic world of the past.

Gaelic football and other gaelic sports of camogie, handball and rounders, all have a more recent history. In football, there are few references before the 1600s, but these are more frequent by the late 1700s.[4] Tipperary, Clare, Wexford, Wicklow, Monaghan, Armagh and Donegal are some of the counties from where there are reports of both hurling and football matches from the early modern period. In addition, by the time of the organisation of Irish sports in the late 19th century, it was probably football as opposed to hurling that was more in need of preservation and cultivation. Even though the Famine of the mid 19th century demoralised the people and almost destroyed the rural social system, in one form or another, gaelic sport survived.

Few comments regarding social or political developments in Ireland can be made without reference to the context of Ireland's relationship with Britain: gaelic sports are no different. Ireland's link with Britain was of a complex colonial nature. Subject to rule from London, this relationship invariably had a vast number of economic, social, cultural and political consequences for the people of the island. One of the results of this domination was that by the late 19th century, as organised sport began to develop in Ireland and much of Europe as a result of the extension of the recreational aspects of contemporary lifestyles, in Ireland regulated sport was largely the preserve of the upper and middle classes. These classes were invariably recognised by the rest of the population as colonist and unionist. Controlled by those of privilege and power, this meant that organised sport in Ireland also served as a vehicle for the promotion of British and Unionist identities. The rest of the population, demoralised and lacking resources, were largely excluded from regulated sport.

Features of life in Ireland considered worthwhile and held in esteem, were often British influenced. Colonial Ireland was multi-faceted in its anglicisation. Sugden and Bairnet write:

> While British domination had always been challenged by the indigenous population, only gradually did this resistance take an overtly nationalist form. Sensitive to the threat of emergent Irish nationalism, the British endeavoured to suppress expressions of gaelic culture. Part of this programme included the discouragement or prohibition of Gaelic games. At the same time distinctively

Anglophile sports, introduced into Ireland by settlers and the agents of the Crown, and encouraged by British landlords, grew in popularity. In addition to these factors the devastating effects of famine pushed Gaelic games nearer to extinction.[5]

As a cultural, sporting and political reaction to this state of affairs, the G.A.A. was founded in 1884.

On All Saints' Day, 1 November 1884, a small group of men met in the billiard room of Miss Hayes Commercial Hotel, Thurles; they formally founded 'The Gaelic Athletic Association for the Preservation and Cultivation of National Pastimes', ever since known as the Gaelic Athletic Association or, more familiarly, the G.A.A..[6]

Michael Cusack, Pat Nally and Maurice Davin among others, became synonymous with the Association's beginnings. Its patrons, Michael Davitt (the founder of the Land League), Charles Stewart Parnell (leader of the Irish Parliamentary Party) and Archbishop Croke (Archbishop of Cashel), became equally associated with the origins of the new organisation. A letter received at the founding of the Association from Archbishop Croke remains an important statement.

…if we continue travelling for the next score years in the same direction that we have been going in for some time past, condemning the sports that were practised by our forefathers, effacing our national features as though we were ashamed of them…we had better at once, and publicly, abjure our nationality, clap hands for joy at sight of the Union Jack and place 'England's bloody red' exultantly above the green…[7]

Croke was also disturbed at the sight of 'youths and young men lolling by the roadside or sneaking about with their hands in their pockets, and with humps on them…'.[8] Croke also made it known that although he supported Irish sports, especially at the expense of the growing British domination of the country, he felt sure that there was room for all recreation: he had no wish to deny other sports and pastimes simply because they were not national. (Michael Davitt stressed that as far as he could interpret, the G.A.A. did not begin with any great political ideal though its aims were national.)

When the Gaelic Association movement was first projected…the idea was national and not political. It was intended to counteract to some extent the denationalising work and tendencies of systems specifically framed to destroy every remnant of our Celtic institutions.[9]

Davitt's involvement with the new Association not surprisingly drew vitriol from the London Daily Telegraph, the paper claiming that a taste for agrarian crime would not be a hindrance to anyone wishing to join the new body.[10]

The idea of political assertion aligning itself with any national project during these years in Ireland seems inevitable. Mullan writes that conflict between native and coloniser over scarce economic resources and occupational life chances:

> established a set of conditions that, by the 1880s, undermined any possibility for the peaceful integration of modern sports.[11]

For Tierney:

> the founding and consolidation of the G.A.A. was part of the social revolution, perhaps its most vital expression. Popular sports, it was said, should be open to all and should be organised by the people not by the ruling class. Here was democracy working its way into rural Ireland, asserting the rights of the Irish people to control their own pastimes...Working class people might watch while the gentry hunted, shot or played tennis, but they must not be allowed to compete. The same applied in athletics, where gentlemen could not imagine themselves having to compete against artisans or agricultural labourers...The G.A.A. hoped to provide a counterblast to the existing class distinction in sport.[12]

(Michael Cusack, at one stage a member of the Fenians, believed that though every social movement in Ireland was to some extent political, the Gaelic Athletic Association was not a political organisation.[13] His great friend and fellow founder of the G.A.A. was certainly a political activist. Patrick Nally, a member of the Irish Republican Brotherhood, one time Connacht representative on the organisation's supreme council, was to die in 1891, incarcerated in Mountjoy prison for his Republican activities. For Holmes, 'Irish nationalism in the nineteenth century revived gaelic football', whilst the founding of the G.A.A. is seen as an important step in the assertion of an Irish national identity.[14] It was the assertion by those not of the colonial set, that they wished to reclaim cultural influence and authority, to begin the process of reviving confidence and pride in being Irish and end the ascendancy of British Protestants over Irish Catholics. Likewise, the Association's founding allowed for the inclusion of the impoverished majority in Ireland in sporting activities: thus the G.A.A. also had a significance in challenging the class domination of sport.

Apart from its political consequences, and its aim of achieving the democratisation of sport in Ireland, the greatest immediate impact of the G.A.A. was the organisation and standardisation of games throughout the country. As a result of this nationalisation of Irish sport, gaelic games were both saved and rejuvenated. The 'movement' took root rapidly throughout the country. Indeed, using the southern version of hurling as his measure, Michael Cusack codified hurling along the lines of which he had known himself as a child in County Clare. For one writer, 'the founding of the G.A.A. caused something of a social revolution'.[15]

Although it would be wrong to see the revival of gaelic games in simply nationalist or political terms, as one writer argues, Cusack and his G.A.A. backers also wished to use the game as a nationalising idiom, a symbolic language of identity filling the void created by the speed of anglicisation. Only a few years after its founding, the G.A.A. was already aligning itself with various groups of evicted tenants as well as the building of nationalist monuments. Its principal backers were those already active in the nationalist political culture of the time, classically the I.R.B. (Irish Republican Brotherhood). Its spread depended on the active support of an increasingly nationalist Catholic middle class — and, as in every country concerned with the invention of tradition, its social constituency especially included journalists, publicans, schoolteachers, clerks, artisans and clerics.[16]

The revival of gaelic sports in Ireland also paralleled the success of the codification of games such as soccer and rugby in Britain. With the shortened working week, its associated concept of 'the weekend', rising spending power and a general organisation of society, the time was ripe for the development and expansion of sporting activity. This sporting revival in Ireland also mirrored events in Australia and the U.S.A. There, Australian Football and American Football (which are much more recent inventions) can be viewed partly as avenues for the construction of national identities.

The growth experienced by the G.A.A. was essentially imitative of the world-wide phenomena whereby various types of ball-games

11

were becoming an integral part of the social fabric. In effect, organisations in North and South America, in Australia, New Zealand, South Africa, India and much of Europe.[17]

Although there are reports of hurling being played in London in 1775, such occurrences were few.[18] However, by 1885 the first G.A.A. club in Britain was founded in Wallsend near Newcastle-on-Tyne, an area of high Irish migration. In a more formal sense, a County Board of the Gaelic Athletic Association was founded in London in 1896 though it was around 1903 before Central Council in Dublin began reporting on gaelic activities in Britain. An early event bridging the Irish Sea occurred in May 1887 when the Celtic Hurling Club of Dublin travelled to Scotland to play Glasgow Cowal Shinty Club at Celtic Park, home of Irish immigrants sporting soccer champions, Celtic Football Club: Cowal winning 11 — 2. The return game was held two months later at which Michael Cussack refereed. Again the Scottish team won, this time 2 — 0.[19] It was not until 1932 that an Irish side gained revenge with a 6 — 1 defeat of the Scottish representatives at the 1932 Tailteann Games in Dublin.

Despite such swift successes, many practical problems faced the G.A.A. Years of internal struggles (financial and personal) and the effects of the nationalist question (including Fenian against constitutionalist and Parnellites versus anti-Parnellites), had their negative effects, although the latter also had a positive influence. A patriotic consciousness provided the Association with more members than might otherwise have been the case, while many activists were certainly motivated by the organisation's political nature. Although patriotic and nationalist, the Association also declared its intention of acting independently of political parties, following its own principles and concentrating on the success and prosperity of the Gaelic Athletic Association.[20] The Association experienced years of slumps and difficulties before it became firmly established. By the early 1900s, it came under the guidance of a set of officials who brought a slow, intermittent, but undoubted revival. This revival also coincided with the general upsurge and participation in cultural activities. As well as the G.A.A. the emergence of the Gaelic League was the most significant feature of this cultural revival. Founded in Dublin in 1893 the Gaelic League has since strived to preserve Irish as a spoken language, to inspire study and publication of existing Irish literature and to promote a modern literature in Irish. In this context of diverse cultural development, gaelic sports gradually began to emerge as a crucial aspect of Irish identity. By 1909, with every county being represented on Central Council, the G.A.A. finally became a genuine national body. In addition, the fortunes of the Association became increasingly tied with those of the growing Irish Ireland bodies of the Gaelic League and Sinn Fein. Indeed, notwithstanding the obvious positive effects that organised sport had on demoralised Ireland and its reflecting on the Association itself, it can be credibly argued that the vibrancy of the G.A.A. derived from the political and cultural mood of the time.

In Ireland, the early years of the 20th century witnessed a new optimism for things Irish. The Association inherently demonstrated opposition to non-Irish sports at the expense of Irish ones, and the first years of the 20th century were important for the development of the 'ban' on the part of the G.A.A. The ban referred to 'foreign' games which were viewed as substantially contributing to the anglicisation of Irish society and were an aspect of the continuing process in the colonisation of the country. As British sports were seen as an extension of British authority, as well as cultural and political domination, to those who engineered the bans, they were viewed as encouraging native games and showing loyalty to native culture. Essentially, this amounted to an organised boycott (participating or spectating) of recognised British games played in Ireland and also a ban on the participation in gaelic games by those considered to be part of the military machine which contributed to the colonisation of the country: members of the British armed forces and the Royal Irish Constabulary (R.I.C.). In relation to the sporting activities which forthwith began to dominate amongst the majority of the people in Ireland, De Burca states:

> These pastimes now passed for ever out of the hands of people like landlords, military and police, who belonged to a class that was opposed both to nationalist political aspirations and to nationalist cultural ideals.[21]

Mullan refers to:

> The pre-GAA Victorian sporting elite — the high professions, the higher echelons of urban commerce, the officer corps of the military

and even the upper echelons of the state civil service, by virtue of a centuries-old system of entrenched Protestant control dating from the Penal Laws — were automatically assigned and isolated to the Anglo-Irish camp of modern sport.[22]

Not for the last time this century, and not in any way restricted to Ireland or the Irish, sport and politics became a repository of national identity. The alliance of the G.A.A. in Ireland with nationalism was a regional variation on an almost universal theme. Two decades before the G.A.A. was born, the Czechoslovakian Sokal Gymnastic Association was formed. The threat of Germanization and the loss of Czech cultural identity motivated leading patriots to revive Czech cultural activities:

> to combine physical education and fitness with specific political objectives — primarily the Czech struggle for national independence...in the face of Austro-Hungarian political and cultural oppression.[23]

For Mandle:

> the use of sport to proclaim national distinctiveness was a British invention: imitations might be made in Melbourne or Tokyo, even in Thurles, Co Tipperary, but imitations they were, not originals.[24]

Combining with the contemporary cultural revival in Ireland, the Irish language movement of the late 19th and early 20th centuries attracted women activists and this also encouraged them to perform an important role in the playing and promotion of gaelic sports. In Ireland, as elsewhere, sport has frequently been a male preserve.[25] However, camogie, a women's version of hurling was developed thus establishing women's contribution to the revival of gaelic sports. The first camogie club was founded and the first recorded game was played in Navan, County Meath in 1904, between the Keatings and Cuchulains of Dublin. Cumann Camogaiochta na Gael was founded at a meeting in Dublin's Gresham Hotel in 1932. In Britain, within two years, twelve camogie clubs existed in London, Manchester and Liverpool, although the game experienced a marked decline by the time of war a few years later.

In 1906 there were seven hundred and fifty G.A.A. clubs' throughout the country, one thousand three hundred and seventeen by the 1927 Congress and almost two thousand, including those in Britain and the U.S.A., by the mid 1930s. By the second decade of the new century, the G.A.A. was firmly established as one of the foremost bodies in Ireland. For Purcell, the G.A.A. and the League combined to reawaken legitimate pride of race, to raise the ideal of nationhood, a concept beyond party and class.[26] The 1920s witnessed a rising wave of popularity for the gaelic sport of handball. During the same period minor gaelic sports competitions were started. At the Easter Congress of 1925, National League games in hurling and football were inaugurated. The same Congress also decided that 'no club be called after a living person or after any political or semi-political organisation'. New peaks in the standard of play, growing attendances and the building of Croke Park in Dublin, also marked important developments. In the 1930s, with the welcome entry of Queen's University in Belfast to the G.A.A. and expansion of third level education in Ireland, university gaelic sports began to develop.

In the years after the 1916 Rising, the G.A.A.'s support for the revolutionary nationalist movement further established it as an important body in Irish society, although the years of the War of Independence and the Civil War clearly also had a detrimental effect on the Association in many areas. Indeed, much of the 1930s had passed before Ulster began to function in a similar way to other provinces: the hostility experienced by the Association in Unionist dominated Northern Ireland proving a severe handicap to the expression of native Irish culture. In fact, it might be argued that it was only after the foundation of the Irish Free State that the G.A.A. was at last in a position to establish itself free of any substantial political or military obstacles. It continued to flourish over the next few decades. Since the 1950s, and the 1960s in particular, the parish G.A.A. club in Ireland has become an important focus for leisure and social activities in the locality. The revival of traditional music and other forms of native culture contributed to a growing strength and significance for the G.A.A. An effective administrative machine and adequate financial resources have also contributed to its importance in Irish life.

At the 1971 Easter Congress held in Belfast, the G.A.A. showed a measure of pragmatism when it viewed the Ban on G.A.A. members attending, promoting and participating in foreign games (rugby, soccer, hockey and cricket) as lacking in contemporary necessity, a feeling that had been emerging for a number of years.

SPORT, CULTURE, POLITICS AND SCOTTISH SOCIETY

Such sports were on the whole viewed as international rather than British and many people in Ireland wished to participate in world-wide games as well as native ones. Ban policy ceased to be seen as a requirement for the preservation and promotion of native games: Crossmaglen delegate, Con Short, moving that the appropriate rule be deleted from the official guide. The success of the removal of the Ban from the constitution and rules of the G.A.A. became obvious almost two decades later when, during the 1980s and 1990s, there was widespread acclaim shown towards the Irish soccer squad which achieved popularity in international soccer competitions. A G.A.A. membership which had hindered removal of the Ban in 1971 may have encountered problems associated with a rigidness inappropriate to the differing era of the 1980s and 1990s. Notwithstanding sporting competition from soccer, this widely acclaimed soccer success also coincided with an era of great progress, classic games and vibrant attendances in gaelic sports. This was particularly so in the province of Ulster, where many sports minded people long displayed a passion for soccer. Nonetheless, throughout the 1990s, a number of All-Ireland champion teams emerged from Ulster and a growing interest in gaelic games in the province revealed to those G.A.A. activists fearful that native sports would lose their appeal in the face of British or global influences, that it was possible to exist and prosper side by side with other sports.

In the 1970s the basic aim of the Association was re-defined as:

> the strengthening of the national identity in a 32-county Ireland through the preservation and promotion of Gaelic games and pastimes.[27]

In 1984 the Gaelic Athletic Association celebrated its centenary. By then it had became a complex organisation which without losing its essential character, was continually adapting to the ways and practices of the mass media and sponsorship. By this time, gaelic games had either been played or continued to be played in countries which traditionally hosted Irish ex-patriot communities; Rhodesia, Argentina, USA, Canada, England, Wales, New Zealand and Scotland. The centenary celebrations of 1984 were to provide a landmark for Gaelic sports. This was particularly the case for some members of the Irish community in Scotland.

16

Notes

1. O Malley, 1979, p. 9.
2. From the Irish Parliament of William 111, National Library of Ireland.
3. Whelan, 1993.
4. de Burca, 1980, p. 5.
5. Sugden and Bairner in Allison (edt), 1986, pp. 90–117.
6. Purcell, 1982, p. 10.
7. G.A.A. Official Guide, 1994.
8. Purcell, p. 46.
9. Michael Davitt on the Celtic invasion of America in 'Sport', Dublin, 25/8/1888, from Healy, 1994.
10. Purcell, p. 48.
11. Mullan, 1995, p. 269.
12. Quoted from Mark Tierney, 'Croke of Cashel', in All-Ireland Final match programme, 17/09/95, p. 78.
13. The Fenians was the name of the mid 19th century Irish organisation who engaged in military struggle against Britain.
14. Holmes, 1994, pp. 81–98.
15. de Burca, p. 26.
16. Whelan, pp. 27–31, also Mullan, pp. 268–289.
17. Rouse, 1993, pp. 333–363.
18. This on a field where the British museum now stands. Irish Post, 3/11/84, p. 4.
19. de Burca, p. 75.
20. Purcell, p. 103.
21. de Burca, p. 100.
22. Mullan, p. 283.
23. Flanagan, 1991, p. 26 in G A Carr, the Spartakiad: Its approach and modification from the mass displays of the Sokol, in the Canadian Journal of history of Sport, vol XV111, May 1987, p. 87.
24. Mandle, 1987, p. 14.
25. Holt, 1996, pp. 231–252.
26. Purcell, p. 123.
27. G.A.A. Rule 1.

CHAPTER 3

THE IRISH IN SCOTLAND

On alien soil like yourself I am here;
I'll take root and flourish of that never fear,
And though I'll be crossed sore and oft by the foes
You'll find me as hardy as Thistle and Rose.
If model is needed on your own pitch you will have it,
Let your play honour me and my friend Michael Davitt.[1]

Immigration: Changing Scotland

Scotland has been home to an immigrant Irish population since
the early 19th century, but particularly since the years of the
exodus from Ireland during an Gorta Mor (the Great Hunger) of
1845–49. One writer, estimates that of those million or more who
departed Ireland during the Famine years, 100,000 came to
Scotland.[2] Over the remaining part of the 19th and early 20th
centuries, tens of thousands more arrived, most invariably settling
among previous generations of immigrants.

Although a number of people who came from the Ulster
province of Ireland were Protestants whose forbears roots lay
mainly in Scotland and who had been part of various plantations
and colonisation periods of Irish/British history, there has been
little research done with regards this movement of people.[3]
Nonetheless, as this group's primary identities have long been a
variety of Scottish, Ulster and British ones, they have also
integrated and assimilated into the wider communities they settled
amongst in Scotland.

By far the largest number of people to migrate from Ireland to
Scotland has been the Catholic Irish. Many have maintained and
employed identities fundamentally different and indeed, often
opposed by and to those identities born of the dominant 'partner'
in Irish — British relations. By the 1990s, from a total population
of approximately five million people, Catholics in Scotland
numbered almost 750,000. A small number of Scots Catholics
existed in Scotland prior to the influx of the Irish (around one per
cent of the total population in 1755), as well as thousands of

immigrant Italian, Polish and Lithuanian Catholics during the 20th century. However, Irish Catholics have been the largest single group to emigrate to Scotland, and in the main, it was the Irish who were to rekindle Catholicism there. Despite indigenous Scots and other European immigrant influences upon Catholicism, for the majority of Catholics in Scotland, particularly in the west central belt where most of them remain concentrated in the late 20th century, many aspects of their cultural, political and religious heritage has been Irish. Nonetheless, Irish identity and influence varies enormously within this community, and like other more indigenous and migrant communities in Scotland, it is not a homogeneous entity.

Although the 1984 G.A.A. centenary celebrations in Ireland were also significant for the Association's membership in Glasgow, the occasion was hardly a celebration of the G.A.A.'s place in Irish culture in west central Scotland or amongst the Irish diaspora there. Indeed, not only was the Gaelic Athletic Association of little relevance to most members of that community, so also were gaelic sports. In 1984 the G.A.A. in Scotland was a tiny moribund organisation which had little bearing on the Irishness of the wider diaspora. By far the dominant sport in Scotland and indeed Britain, was football, or soccer as it is often called among the gaelic fraternity. Traditionally, in Ireland soccer was largely limited to Ulster or to a few urban centres in the Republic. Outside of Ireland soccer attracted the Irish as it did many communities around the globe. In 1984 the G.A.A. in Scotland had a presence, but it was only as a small organisation which few within the Irish community were aware of. Of course, the G.A.A. had taken many decades before it finally began to make a major impact upon Irish society, and this was undoubtedly a factor for the Association's long trek to establishment in Scotland.

The 1851 census figure for the Irish included Protestants from Ulster. The figures for that year found that around seven per cent of the Scottish population had been born in Ireland: just over 200,000.[4] The vast majority of these were Irish Catholics. By 1901, there were almost 400,000 Catholics who were Irish born or who were second or third generation Irish in Scotland. Although some present day 'Irish' can trace a presence in Scotland for five or even six generations, those same people can also claim more recent forebears in that they also have a partner, parent or grandparent who are of a later wave of immigrants. These more recent immigrants almost inevitably marrying into the existing Irish community, thus often reinforcing or strengthening previously lost or abandoned familial links to their country of origin. However, the main point in noting such vast numbers of Irish in Scotland prior to the 20th century, is to acknowledge that they had a presence there before the Gaelic Athletic Association in Ireland was founded and before it had found its place even in Irish society. This is crucial to understanding why it was soccer that many Irish in Scotland turned to for expressing themselves culturally, especially through sport.

Although all the counties of Ireland's provinces are represented among Irish immigrants coming to Scotland, a majority of later immigrants almost certainly originated from Ulster's counties, north Leinster, or of Mayo and other northerly counties of the province of Connacht. This is also relevant to the strength of the G.A.A. in Scotland in that many of these were the same areas in which the Association struggled most in Ireland. De Burca states that in the mid 1890s Connacht and Ulster were lost to the Association.[5] By 1900, both provinces remained almost entirely outside the G.A.A., though gaelic games continued to be played in an unorganised fashion. At the 1892 annual convention, actually held the following year, just three counties were represented. Only three counties contested the 1893 hurling championship while six competed to become football champions. Even today, the present hurling core region in Ireland is based largely on Cork, Tipperary and Kilkenny, though other counties like Limerick, Clare, Galway, Offaly, Laois, Waterford and Wexford also have strong hurling traditions. Nonetheless, even within these counties, the game can be designated by virtue of the local geography: often it is not whole counties but parts of counties in which the game is viewed as intrinsic. In parts of Ulster's north eastern counties Down and Antrim, the game is also crucial to local culture. Despite this strength, and as already noted, it was the 1930s before the G.A.A. began to have the significance for Irish life in Ulster that it had in the rest of the country.

In addition, much of the population of Ireland had been demoralised throughout the years of colonialism and particularly as a consequence of the Great Famine of the 19th century. Kinealy believes that the price paid by the Irish for the Famine was:

20

'privation, disease, emigration, mortality and an enduring legacy of disenchantment'.[6] Dr Douglas Hyde, later to become the first President of Ireland, concluded:

> The Famine destroyed everything. Poetry, music and dancing stopped. Sport and pastimes disappeared. And when times improved, those things never returned as they were.[7]

Immigrants from Ireland were often much too concerned with surviving in an alien and hostile environment and of not drawing attention to themselves. Crucially, many left Ireland some years before a new era of confidence in Irish cultural activities began to make a social and political impact. The greatest influence on indigenous Irish games becoming widespread among the Irish in Scotland came in the shape of a 'foreign' sport, soccer. The social conditions that the Irish experienced in Scotland meant that the G.A.A. had a limited impact upon the immigrant community, while another and unique form of Irish identity was constructed in Scotland as a response to those conditions.

Notes

1. Wilson, 1988, p. 21.
2. Handley, 1964.
3. For existing research see McFarland, 1986 and Walker and Gallagher, 1990.
4. Therefore also a figure which underestimated the Irish presence because it did not consider their offspring.
5. de Burca, 1980, p. 63.
6. Kinealy, 1994, p. 359.
7. Irish Post, 2/9/95, p. 8.

CHAPTER 4

THE G.A.A. IN SCOTLAND: 1897–1916

Mind will rule and muscle yield,
In Senate, ship and field;
When we've skill our strength to wield,
Let us take our own again.[1]

Founding years

There is a dearth of records relating to many aspects of the Irish in Scotland. Even today, there are few studies of that community's historical, sociological, political or contemporary experience. In terms of the G.A.A. in Ireland, the Associations own records initially lack depth and organisation. In addition, due to the political situation in Ireland at the time and the resultant semi-secrecy within the G.A.A., many of the Association's early records were unwritten or are unreliable.

Nonetheless, what is clear is that by the turn of the 20th century, the G.A.A. was making progress amongst the Irish abroad as well as at home. In addition, in the early period, the gaelic sporting revival conducted by the G.A.A. was centred on the sport of hurling.[2] By the mid-1890s New York had some twenty G.A.A. clubs operating. In England in 1896, the G.A.A. was founded by the ex-patriot community, which was followed in 1900 by the organisation of a provincial council. Reflecting the sense of patriotism often felt by gaelic minded people, one of the first clubs' affiliated to the G.A.A. in London was the Robert Emmet's club of Marlybone. The idea of calling a club after a perceived patriot has been a hallmark of G.A.A. clubs since the founding of the Association. When the Tuam Krugers Club was founded in County Galway around 1900, the club's name amounted to a statement with regards 'British colonialism' and the Boer War underway in South Africa, as well too as a clear identification with Britain's enemy at that time.[3]

In late 19th and early 20th century Ireland, politics was an intricate part of the G.A.A. In Britain it was a similar story. Such politics were frequently more likely to do with ideas regarding identity, and was a reaction to the negative state of things Irish and the dominance of things British in Ireland. Although political activists were to become crucial to the development and shaping of the Association, many members of the G.A.A. also attempted to keep their distance from party political and institutional politics. At the same time, the involvement of many Irish Republican Brotherhood (I.R.B.) members with the G.A.A. meant that revolution was also a component of much G.A.A. thinking and this was exemplified in London with Michael Collins and others like him.

Collins was secretary of the Geraldines G.A.A. Club in London, treasurer of the London County Board, and was eventually to rise to national and international prominence as one of the main participants in the pivotal years of the struggle for Irish independence, 1916 to 1922. He became director of intelligence in Ireland during the War of Independence and chief Irish plenipotentiary during the Treaty debate in London. Sam Maguire, whose name the All-Ireland football trophy bears, was born to a Church of Ireland family in Mallabraga, near Dunmanway, County Cork in 1879. He was an outstanding footballer who played for Hibernians in London (winning four championships in a row, 1901–1904) and who captained the London County team to three All-Ireland finals between 1900 and 1903. He was elected Chairman of the London County Board in 1907. A member of the Gaelic League, as Major General and Chief Intelligence Officer of the Irish Republican Army in Britain, 'during the war of independence, all major republican operations in Britain were largely under the control of Sam Maguire'.[4] Liam MacCarthy, who was to give his name to the All-Ireland Hurling Championship Trophy, also played gaelic sports in Britain. He became treasurer of the London County in 1895 and President in 1898. MacCarthy was 2nd generation Irish, born in London of County Cork parents who had immigrated to England in 1851. It was MacCarthy who recruited Michael Collins to the republican movement in 1909.

In the late 19th century there was also significant Irish political activity among the immigrant community in the west of Scotland. Glasgow, Lanarkshire and their environs contained noteworthy associations of the Irish National League then the primary body advocating Irish home rule. Indeed, one of the largest branches of the Home Rule movement in Britain in the 1890s was to be found in the Lanarkshire town of Coatbridge, which was also 'able in one year to donate more funds to the League's treasury than almost any of the great cities'.[5]

In 1895, one of the main Irish Catholic newspapers of the time, *The Glasgow Examiner*, printed a letter which complained at the lack of Irish cultural activity corresponding to the gaelic revival in Ireland.[6] A positive response was forthcoming. The same year, the William O'Brien Gaelic Class was formed which became a branch of the Gaelic League before the year had ended.[7] This year thus marks the establishment of the Gaelic League in Glasgow, only two years after its founding in Dublin. Over the next few years the Gaelic League underwent a significant growth among the Irish communities of greater Glasgow and Lanarkshire.

The first record of a G.A.A. club in Scotland is to be found in 1897. *The Glasgow Examiner* carried news that:

> a large and enthusiastic meeting of young Irishmen of the city was held in the Young Ireland Hall…for the purpose of forming a branch of the Gaelic Athletic Association in Glasgow

It was agreed by those present that the Red Hugh O'Neill Gaelic Athletic Club be set up to include all branches of Irish national pastime — hurling, football, running, jumping, boxing, and dumbbell and Indian club exercises, etc.[8] The club was to be non-sectarian but membership was restricted to respectable young men of Irish birth or parentage, and of good moral character. The emphasis on such a strong Irish lineage reflecting the strength of that particular category within the immigrant community.

It is likely that it was the politically active amongst the Irish community who gave birth to the 'Red Hugh' Club. The location for engagements was well established as a place for nationalist meetings and there seems to have been some overlap in membership of those of the Irish National League and the new club: John Brolly and Joseph McFaulds (or McFalls) being involved in both bodies. Tom Fergie of the Ormond Club was designated trainer and Mr P Honeyman became president. Nonetheless, although the club was reported as being in regular training and preparing for a match against a London side, reports of hurling activity in Glasgow quickly died.

Contributing to difficulties regarding gaelic sporting activities among the ex-patriot community was an emphasis on soccer. As was the case all over Britain and in much of the Empire, sport was to have a growing social and cultural importance during this period and it regularly made the front pages of newspapers. The 'Athletic Notes' column in *The Examiner* was written by Celtic soccer official John McLaughlin and his emphasis on the club helped promote Celtic amongst the Irish. Other sports such as cycling and athletics received occasional mention in the *The Examiner*, but with a spectrum of sporting events regularly organised at the home of Celtic, and with these sports dominating the relevant newspaper columns, gaelic sports faced an uphill struggle. Few, if any sporting reports emerged from Ireland itself. *The Examiner*, was a paper which reported on Irish affairs and events in a way which strongly suggests that the immigrant community remained closely tied with their homeland: they clearly constituted, 'the Irish in Scotland'. An *Examiner* account in early 1897 recognised the erecting of a replica cross of Cashel to the memory of Dr Croke: he was seen as, 'one of the most valiant and strenuous defenders of the birthrights of the Irish people'. Despite the high sentiments, this report remains one of the few references to the early G.A.A. in Ireland on the part of the Irish Catholic press in Scotland.[9]

Among the immigrant community, Irish political and cultural activities were plentiful. The Irish National League, Irish Independent League, Ancient Order of Hibernians and the Irish National Foresters, added to the plethora of Catholic bodies as well as Celtic Football Club, meant that by the end of the 19th century, being Irish in Scotland had an array of outlets. The first signs of the gaelic revival taking place in Ireland having an impact upon the Irish in Scotland, is reflected in the regular Gaelic League columns in *The Examiner* newspaper from August 1896 onwards. By 1897, there was seventeen branches of the League in Ireland, four in England as well as one in Glasgow: the latter based in St Francis Parish in the east of the city. In 1899 Padraic Pearse visited Glasgow's League to encourage its growth. On his next visit in 1902 he spoke admiringly of the League in the city.

> Then there was only one branch of the League in the city — the Glasgow branch — which was then in its infancy. Now there were a dozen branches and outside London with its vast Irish population,

25

there was no centre where the language movement had made such progress as in Glasgow.[10]

Pearse was welcomed to Scotland by Glasgow born Hugh McAleese, who along with his brothers, Cormac and Charles, were also present at the founding of the first branch of the League in Glasgow.[11] In relation to the growth of the Gaelic League in Scotland, Handley informs us that:

> By the turn of the century, the Gaelic movement in the West of Scotland had seventeen branches in the Glasgow district. Later years saw the establishment of centres in Paisley, Blantyre, Motherwell, Hamilton, Wishaw, Coatbridge, Carfin, Renton, Kilsyth, Barrhead, Denny, Johnstone, Dumbarton, Ayr, Port Glasgow and Greenock. In the east of Scotland, classes were opened for a time at Dundee, Edinburgh and Leith...taught by Glasgow Gaels...All labour was voluntary and unpaid...[12]

Over the course of the first decades of the new century, the expansion of the Gaelic League in west central Scotland was to be particularly significant in relation to the evolution of Gaelic Athletic Clubs.

The dominance of Celtic Football Club amongst Irish cultural and social activities was shown in 1900 when it was reported that there existed the possibility of a new Irish sporting club emerging in Glasgow and which would appeal to the followers of Celtic and Hibernian, the latter being Irish immigrants' soccer representatives in the east of the country. The threat to Celtic was discounted on the basis that the only club that could possibly emerge in the financial climate of the times would be an Irish hurling team. Reflecting how little competition on the part of gaelic sports was perceived by the soccer minded Irish in Glasgow, one of the important members involved in the first few years of Celtic Football Club was William McKillop M.P., who actually gifted a cup to the Armagh G.A.A. in 1907. Regarding the issue of another Irish sporting club in Glasgow John McLaughlin stated in *The Examiner*, that:

> Such a club would in no way be antagonistic to the Celts. Indeed, the Celts have already shown their interests in the Gaelic game by bringing over two or three hurling teams from Ireland. If the Gaelic enthusiasts in Glasgow succeeded in forming their teams we have no doubt that the Celts would not be averse to giving the use of the

Paradise for the purpose of an exhibition game. Such hurling clubs already exist in London and Manchester and are affiliated to the Central Executive of the Gaelic Athletic Association in Dublin.[13]

Although slow in emerging, the growth of the Irish Ireland movement of the time was reflected among the Irish diaspora in Scotland. In Ireland, Irish Irelanders hoped to reverse many of the features of British influenced colonial Ireland and to reinstate what they perceived as more native ways, including a revival of the Irish language and gaelic sports. Amongst the diaspora, Irish Irelanders wished to promote a similar set of values and cultural practices though these intentions were clearly affected by differing circumstances.

By early 1901 the Rapparees Hurling Club was formed in Glasgow, a club which became one of the most significant of all clubs founded over the course of the 20th century. One of the founders of the new club, Proinnsia O Maonaigh, suggested that the club should be called after his former club in Dublin, also the Rapparees. Initial training took place at Woodend Park, Jordanhill, the ground of Jordanhill Football Club. A close association with the Gaelic League in the city is apparent in that subsequent sporting activities were reported alongside League activities. Hurling meetings in Glasgow were also held in the League Rooms in the National Halls, at 52 Castle Bank Street, Partick.

Links with the Gaelic League are further evidenced in an overlap in membership: John Keegan, T McGettrick, D and P Cronin were some of the members of both the Partick Branch of the Glasgow Gaelic League and the Rapparees Hurling Club. George Shorten from Ballingeary County Cork, an influential figure in initiating the Rapparees Club, was also a Gaelic Leaguer though he was to return to Cork in early 1902. Although some gaelic football was played by the Rapparees as well as efforts to begin a regular team, hurling continued to dominate. The first game participated in by the Rapparees Club was against the Caledonian Shinty Club at the latter teams ground at Possilpark, Glasgow, in May 1901: the Irish side being beaten 5-2 by the Glasgow team.[14]

In March of 1901 the Whiteinch Hurling Club, The Faughs, was formed from the Whiteinch Branch of the Gaelic League. Govandale Park, the ground of the Benburb soccer club, became the new team's home ground. The following month *The Examiner* reported that a new club, Eire Og, had been formed in Port

connection between celt soccer + gaa
shared grounds

27

Glasgow near Greenock. At the first match at Battery Park, Greenock, between the Rapparees (the winners) and Eire Og, both teams finished the day's festivities by singing the rallying songs of the League. A few months later the Cuchulin Hurling Club began in Polmadie area of the city. In mid 1901, at a meeting in the Grand National Halls, the Rapparee Hurling Club decided to affiliate to the Gaelic Athletic Association in Dublin.[15] By the middle of the following year, such were the numbers attending the Rapparees activities that it was decided to form another club from the excess of players. In May 1902, at a meeting in St Patrick's School, Coatbridge, the Patrick Sarsfield Branch of the Gaelic League also initiated a hurling club.

In August a match took place between the newly formed Sarsfield Club of Coatbridge and the Rapparees. After the visitors had been taken on tour of local Catholic schools and Churches, a match commenced in the West End Park at Langloan, a well known Irish quarter of the town. Around three thousand people attended the match finally won by the visiting club.

In March 1903, the Carfin Branch of the Gaelic League, along with local priest Father John O Dea of County Clare, organised a hurling match in the village between the Rapparees and Cuchulains. This match took place with the intention of advertising the sport and initiating a team in the area. By now the Rapparees were considered to be champion hurlers of Scotland. A few months later a Carfin team was successfully started. Called Faug-an-ballaghs (later referred to as Fag-an-Bealach), they played their first fixture against another Lanarkshire side, Wishaw Shamrocks. This game is noted for the first references in Scotland to goals and points being scored (some previous games involved goals only), a factor relevant to the developing ties with Dublin and the standardisation of the rules of the game. This particular game was followed by a gaelic football match between local Irish miners and railwaymen, won by the former with a one goal advantage.[16] May 1903 witnessed a hurling match in Carfin between the local club and Patrick Sarsfields from Coatbridge. Both clubs' links with the Gaelic League were apparent in this fixture with around one hundred Gaelic Leaguers accompanying the hurling team from Coatbridge to watch the game in Carfin.

By mid 1903 developments in Irish gaelic sports in Scotland began to gain momentum. This year marks the first mention in

GAA in Scotland, was acknowledge by GAA headquarters C.P.

records at Croke Park regarding gaelic sport in Scotland: Central Council of the G.A.A. receiving 'an application from the Scotland County Board for permission to have two representatives from every club on the Central Committee'.[17] With five clubs now affiliated to Dublin, by June there was talk of forming a county board, 'which shall have full jurisdiction over all matches played by affiliated clubs in Scotland'.[18] This was achieved before the month had ended. The clubs represented at the first meeting of the Glasgow and West of Scotland County Board were; Rapparees (delegates — Murray and Corbett), Wishaw Shamrocks (Moran and McLaughlin), Fag-an-bealachs, Carfin (O'Neill and O'Timmoney), Patrick Sarsfields, Coatbridge (McCourt and Graham), Finn MacCumhails, Anderston and Partick (O'Brien and Dougherty), Hibernians, Pollockshaws (McDade and Gallagher) and Cuchulains, Polmadie (O'Connor and Hayes). By the time of the first meeting of the new county the following week, the anticipated affiliation by clubs from Greenock and Shettleston took place.[19] Nine clubs thus formed the first county in Scotland in 1903 and Lanarkshire based Rev John O Dea of County Clare was unanimously chosen as president. By July of the same year an organised hurling league was underway.

The first county in Glasgow had high expectations. By August 1903 it was noted by the exiles in Scotland that London had won the All-Ireland hurling title from Cork suggesting such a feat was also possible for Scotland a few years hence. With a good year behind them, the Board in Scotland felt themselves to be preparing for the 1904 All-Ireland Championship. Although there were a number of players with no hurling background playing the game, at the time there were also a number of skilled hurlers in the west of Scotland. In late 1903, *The Star* observed that for a forthcoming game between the Rapparees and Wishaw Shamrocks:

> As the majority of the members of both teams have fought and gained honours in many a Gaelic athletic gathering in the old country, a good hurling match should be the result.

The teams taking part were:

> Rapparees: Hennessy, Murray, Moroney, Cody, J Ryan, P Ryan, Jas Ryan, Laffan, Linehan, O'Flynn, Devitt, O'Carroll, W Nagle, D Nagle, Shanahan, Herbert and Reid.

Shamrocks: O'Mahoney, Mullane, Regan, Nagle, O'Kelly, McGlynn, O'Brien, Dilworth, Crilly, O'Callaghan, Smith, Murray, Collins, O'Dougherty, Green, O'Kelly and O'Neill.[20]

The surnames of the participants suggests that a number of those playing the game probably originated from the hurling counties of Munster and the southern half of Ireland. One historian believes that many of the Rapparees had played with Tipperary and Cork teams before immigrating to Scotland.[21] Numerous references had been made over the previous few years to Tipperary players in particular making their mark on the game in Glasgow. In one match between Sarsfields of Coatbridge and the Rapparees, Delaney took part for the Glasgow team: Delaney being a former Tipperary hurler who had latterly played with Southern Rovers in Dublin.

Progress proceeded and by the end of the momentous year of 1903, it was reported that two junior hurling clubs had been formed in Lanarkshire: Desmonds in Wishaw and The Dalcassians in Carfin. There was also talk of clubs starting in Hamilton and Motherwell and even of another county board in Lanarkshire. By early 1905, the G.A.A. in Scotland had acquired the status of a 'Province', which had the same rights and privileges as the others of Ulster, Connacht, Munster, Leinster and London.

The promotion of the game in Scotland continued apace. During March 1904 the Brian Boroimhe (Brian Boru) Gaelic Club from Blantyre in Lanarkshire affiliated to the main body in Scotland. Later in the year, the Blantyre Club played their first official football match against Sarsfields from Coatbridge in the latter town's Dunbeth Park.[22] By the middle of the following year a match was reported between Patrick Sarsfields of Coatbridge and St Margarets of Airdrie.[23] Around the same time, there was word of gaelic clubs functioning in Cleland (Lambh Dearg) and Shieldmuir, Motherwell (Lord Edwards).[24]
The Star reported that:

During the coming year there will be plenty opportunities for any Gael who holds the welfare of his national, manly pastime of any account in the reformation of the "sea divided gael" into a compact and self-reliant nation to take a true man's part.[25]

The theme of true gaels exclusively playing the sports of their ancestors was of course a recurrent one for those involved in gaelic pastimes. One gaelic activist in Scotland went so far as to criticise the Irish and Catholic bodies (in this case the Robert Emmet Club and the William O Brien Branch of the United Irish League) who played soccer amongst themselves or faced other clubs for that purpose. For this particular writer the only way to become a real athlete was to play gaelic games.[26]

In June 1905, Scotland and England played a hurling fixture in the city of Liverpool.[27] Ryan, Lanigan and Fitzpatrick were three of the players from Scotland who participated in a game won by the gaels from England. As England's gaelic representatives from London (whose chairman was Liam McCarthy) had won the All-Ireland only two years previously, the team from Scotland reckoned they had achieved much in a short space of time. As a reflection of this progress, in early 1906 a gaelic football league also got underway. Both hurling and football were played in a special meeting between Ulster and Scotland in Belfast in 1905. At Easter time three years later, an England versus Scotland fixture was arranged for London.

The new provincial board of Scotland was represented by Messrs Cunningham and Fitzpatrick of Lanarkshire and Messrs Fitzgibbon and Flynn from Glasgow. They also elected Coatbridge representative, John McCourt, as president. McCourt was an energetic Irish activist who was also involved in the Hibernians, the League of the Cross and the Irish National Foresters among other bodies. Despite being Lanarkshire based, McCourts own club, Patrick Sarsfield's, were affiliated to the Glasgow part of the province, though this is likely to have been as a result of the Lanarkshire Coatbridge club having been in existence prior to the formation of the Lanarkshire board.[28] By early 1906, the Lanarkshire County had nine clubs in affiliation, including gaelic football clubs, the Sons of Erin from Carfin and St Patricks from Wishaw. Indeed, the board hoped for a further expansion for the Association in Scotland. Its members especially looked to the Irish Irelanders of Lanarkshire and to the Ancient Order of Hibernians who at a convention in Dublin in 1905 pledged its members to support gaelic games as well as the Irish language.

The continued expansion of Irish cultural activities in west central Scotland was reflected in the decision of the Provincial Board to compete in both the All-Ireland provincial football and hurling championships of 1906. Over the course of the next few years, football or hurling clubs sprang up in Springburn Glasgow (Clan na Ghaeldhilge), Coatbridge (Eire Og, hurling) and Kinning Park Glasgow (Lambh Dearg, football). Mr Denis Brogan, 'a self-made Donegal tailor',[29] and a well known member of the Gaelic League, presided over the fund raising gathering which helped launch the latter club.

By April 1908, *The Star* reported that young Irishmen had met to form a gaelic football and hurling club at the Hibernian Hall in Kerse Lane, Falkirk.[30] The founding committee, included Messrs:

W Burke, J Nagle, M Dongan, J O Neill, J Devine, W Byre, P McCann, W McMonagle, P McClosky, M Murphy, P McBride, S Kellagher, P Gormerly and F Gilhooly.

In the same year efforts were made to begin a hurling club in Dumbarton.[31] Other Glasgow gaelic clubs such as the Cavan Slashers (who later joined with Eire Ogs in Glasgow) and Fianna Eireann, were also mentioned in the gaelic columns of the Irish paper, thus showing the growing strength of gaelic sport in Scotland during this period.

The year 1906 was eventful for Irish gaels in Scotland. In Lanarkshire, the first ever hurling championship was won by the Brian Boru Club from Blantyre.

Table 4.1
Lanarkshire Hurling Championship 1906

	play	won	lost	for	against	points
Brian Boru	7	7	0	26	9	14
Lord Edwards	6	4	2	22	14	8
Shamrocks	5	2	3	20	12	4
Fag-an-Bealagh	7	2	5	12	19	4
Lambh Dearg	7	1	6	9	20	2

The same year, Fag-an-Bealagh (Sons of Erin) from Carfin won the first football championship, though overall, it was Glasgow which continued to dominate. Before a crowd of over fifteen hundred people in the provincial hurling championship held at Shawfield Park, the home of Clyde Football Club, Lanarkshire's representatives Brian Boru's were beaten by the experienced Rapparees Club.

Glasgow's experience was again reflected in the provincial championship of that year. Earlier, in a challenge match in

England, a strong representative team from Scotland beat Tyneside 5:12 to 2:5. For the Ulster (Antrim) versus Scotland (Glasgow) 1905 All-Ireland hurling quarter final match held in August 1906, eleven members of the Rapparees Club were chosen, four from the Cuchulains Club and one each from Lord Edwards and Shamrocks of Wishaw. However, complaints that travelling such a significant distance to the match in Ireland had a negative effect upon the Scottish based team could not change the reality of a narrow defeat: Antrim winning 3:13 to 3:11. Around the same time Leinster (Kilkenny) defeated the English representatives (Lancashire) 3:21 to 0:5.

In early 1907, the Glasgow and Lanarkshire county boards amalgamated to form a new provincial committee. The following year, St Mark's Parish of Carntyne (now Shettleston) in Glasgow formed the first handball team within gaelic circles in Scotland. The first record of a handball game being played amongst the gaelic fraternity dates from mid 1908: St Marks beating the resolute and capable Rapparees Club in the contest.[32] Games in Ireland or with visiting clubs from Ireland also began to take place. The Lambh Dearg's from Kinning Park paid a visit to Belfast in September 1908 to play the Seaghan an Diomais Club. The match, played at Seaghan's Park on the Whiterock Road was won 1:12 to 1:8 by the home side. The closeness of the result reflected the high standard of play of the Scottish based team: the home side apparently having the pick of the best players in Belfast for the match. The following year the Rapparees visited Nenagh in Tipperary and Cork to play local sides in hurling challenge matches. For the 1908 All-Ireland Championships, London were chosen to represent Britain in football and Scotland in the hurling competition. London lost to Dublin in the final while Scotland failed to travel for its semi-final against Tipperary.[33] In 1910 in hurling, Glasgow defeated Antrim 1:13 to 0:7 in the quarter-final of the All-Ireland Hurling Championship. The county subsequently lost to Dublin, 6:6 to 5:1 in the semi-final played at Jones's Road, Dublin.[34]

In early 1909, the G.A.A. in Scotland reflected its concern with the advance of the Irish language when it joined the debate on the use of Irish in Irish universities. In January of that year the Province passed a resolution which was sent to the secretary of Coisde Gnotha, Gaelic League, Dublin.

> That we, the Scottish Provincial Council of the Gaelic Athletic Association, demand that the Irish language, both oral and written, be made an essential subject for matriculation and up to the point where specialisation begins in the new universities.[35]

Around this time gaelic football began to come more to the fore among some small sections of the Irish community in the west of Scotland. The first ever league competition was held during 1909 and was only decided on the final day of the season. Eire Og from Coatbridge beat Kinning Park's Lambh Dearg in front of a crowd of three hundred spectators. The Coatbridge team which won the first league title was:

> Plunkett, Carvil, Harknett, Wroe, Walsh, Carville, Maguire, Kelly, O Neill, Kernan, Darcy, Byrne, O Brien, Hughes, Devlin, Dunn and Carolan.

To the credit of the Coatbridge representatives, the Star reported:

> It would be but natural for the good Gaels of Coatbridge to feel proud of their achievement, but they carry their honours modestly, as befits men who are good footballers and good hurlers and who take an active practical interest in every phase of the Irish movement as regards the Irish language and industrial revival.[36]

The Irishness of Coatbridge's immigrant population was frequently to attract positive comment from other members of the Irish community. Belfast MP Joseph Devlin visited Scotland during the St Patrick's celebrations the following year. When Devlin visited Coatbridge, Dr Charles O Neill, the Coatbridge MP who represented South Armagh, was encouraged to welcome Mr Devlin to a United Irish League meeting in the town's Theatre Royal. O Neill commented that Devlin:

> would not need any pressure to force him to come there to witness such a demonstration of Irish power and loyalty.[37]

In November 1911, at a meeting in Upper O Connell Street, Dublin, Central Council reported that Scotland was still making steady progress in the formation of gaelic clubs and that additional clubs had affiliated to the relevant committee in Ireland during the year. However, the many positive signs of a gaelic revival amongst the ex-patriot community in Scotland was continually being qualified by set backs. For almost two years there was little official hurling or football activity within the community. An article in *The Star* stated:

> Bad as things are, there is no reason why the G.A.A. should not again be a vigorous body amongst the Irishmen in Scotland and particularly among those congregated in Glasgow and throughout the West of Scotland.[38]

It appears that the Rapparees were the only club credibly sustaining itself at the time. *The Star* newspaper reported that despite the many hundreds of hurlers in the area, a lack of opposition was in danger of rendering the club 'blue mouldy'.[39] Gaelic sports in west central Scotland did not suffer from a lack of Irishness, for Irish activity remained plentiful; the Irish Forresters, the Irish National League, Celtic Football Club and the Hibernians, with thirty four divisions in the central belt of Scotland, were the clearest signs of Irish activity. Irish identity during this period simply did not translate into a vibrant G.A.A. As was the case in parts of Ireland, the G.A.A. in Scotland struggled to acquire the status and vibrancy required for its good health and promotion.

Nonetheless, throughout these years there were many positive periods as well as those which were handicapped by a lack of activity. By the middle of 1912, Eire Og Hurling Club in Coatbridge was again recruiting, practising and organising. The occasional challenge match was taking place and there was newspaper speculation of clubs being rekindled in Wishaw, Whiteinch (Glasgow) and Greenock. The Owen Roe O Neill Gaelic Football Club was founded in Coatbridge in late 1912. The Club held an inaugural function in a hall in the town's Coatdyke area: forty members signed up and the evening was rounded off with the singing of the emerging unofficial Irish national anthem, 'A Nation Once Again'. Around the same time Coatbridge's Eire Og met Sarsfields of Greenock in the first match in the Jersey Hurling Tournament. Although Wishaw Shamrocks failed to field in the tournament, matches did take place and the final was played in November of that year with Greenock's Sarsfields being the victors over the Rapparees. The final teams were:

> Sarsfields: J O Conner (captain), D West, J West, J O Callaghan, S Tabb, C McCarthy, J Dillon, D O Brien, W Perry, T Hirshaw, M O Leary, D O Leary, E Flynn.

Rapparees: W Hennessy, L Hudson, D O Donnoghue, H Ryan, F Mooney, M Minogue, D Minogue, J Minogue, P MacKay, J McCarthy, J Darragh, M Fitzgerald, R Morrisey.[40]

During November 1912, the *Cork Free Press* reported a match in 'Bonny Scotland' noting the predominance of Hurlers from County Cork's Passage West, who played in the Greenock Sarsfields team and, were 'keeping the cult of the caman well to the fore' among the Irish in Scotland. The local Cork economy had been suffering and the Free Press reported that the young men were now employed as apprentices at the Greenock shipyards. The paper lamented the need for its young men to leave home and also the demise of the club they once played for.

> All veteran South-East Cork Leaguers will be specifically interested, as it will show that though the famous old Passage club is non est at present, its members are keeping the memories of the dear old days green by indulging in the home pastime.

The newspaper hoped that better times, 'when the trade of Passage will revive', would allow the young men to return to their native Cork.[41]

The year 1913 was a landmark for the Irish hurling and football gaels in the west of Scotland. In April G.A.A. clubs began to meet again as a provincial board. The Scottish Province's representative, Eamonn O Fhlionn, won an assurance at a Central Council meeting in Dublin that the 1913 All-Ireland quarter-final provincial hurling match involving Scotland would, for the first time, be played in Glasgow. This was in response to previous complaints from members in Scotland that constant travel difficulties were hindering their chances of progress in the competition. It was also part of an initiative on the part of the G.A.A. authorities in Ireland to attempt 'to boost the game in Britain'.[42]

The following month the Province announced its biggest news to date. In June, previous winners of a number of All-Ireland Hurling titles, Kilkenny, would visit Glasgow to play against a select of members in Scotland. This provided the Scottish Board with a major incentive for both selling the game and for installing a degree of enthusiasm and anticipation into clubs which had until recently been struggling to field regular sides. Training and practice matches became more common as the Provincial selectors looked over players with a view to picking the best for the match with Kilkenny.

During May, the Rapparees beat the previous years winners, Sarsfields of Greenock, to lift the Hurling Championship of Scotland.[43] When the spectacle of the Scottish County versus Kilkenny took place at Celtic Park on the 21st June 1913, the supremacy of the Rapparees side in Scotland was reflected in their having seven players included for the match. Those who represented both teams on this occasion were:

Kilkenny. J Power (Mooncoin), J Keoghan (Tullaroan), J Rochford (Three Castles), M Garrigle (Erin's Own, Kilkenny City), D Kennedy (Tullaroan), P Lanigan (Erin's Own), T MacCormick (Erin's Own), P Clohossay (Tullaroan), D Doherty (Mooncoin), S Walton (Tullaroan/Captain), M Doyle (Mooncoin) and J Kelly (Mooncoin). Reserves, J J Brennan (Erin's Own) and D Welsh (Mooncoin).

Scottish County. M Morrohan (Rapparees, Glasgow), L Hartnett (Eire Og, Coatbridge), D Donoghue (Rapparees), B O Neill (Wishaw Shamrock's/Captain), J McNulty (Rapparees), F Stephens (Shamrock's), J Tabb (Sarsfields, Greenock), E Flynn (Sarsfields), J Phelan (Eire Og), W Fitzgerald (Rapparees), W Dwyer (Rapparees), O Connor (Sarsfields), J McCarthy (Rapparees) and P MacGearailt (Sarsfields). Reserves, P Dwyer, McDonnell and R Welsh.

The Kilkenny side were well represented by players from the Tullaroan and Mooncoin clubs, two of the strongest sides in the County, who played in the first Kilkenny championship in 1887. Further, these years marked a particularly successful time for the Kilkenny team which won seven All-Ireland titles in a ten year period and which also won the championship the same year the team played at Celtic Park.

The sports reporter for *The Glasgow Star*, 'Man In The Know', Tom Maley (brother of the Celtic manager, Willie), enthused at the wonderful spectacle which took place at Celtic park. Maley was even taken by the appearance of the Rory Oge O More Pipe Band who the Celtic directors arranged to appear again at Celtic Park the following August. Although *The Star* was dominated by soccer reports, particularly those pertaining to the Celtic club, 'The Man In The Know' was clearly taken by the exhibition hurling match. Writing in the following week's *Star*, Maley wrote:

The game itself was a revelation to those of us who look upon football as the last word in competitive sport…The players covered more ground than any football fifteen could do in the allotted time and space; their ambidextrous strokes were a combination of golf, baseball, cricket, and tennis swings, and all the time eye and muscle had to synchronise, the ball timed with the utmost accuracy, and sent either to a waiting comrade or as near the opponents' goal as possible.

Although Maley enthused about the game, and despite his remarks being indicative of the struggle which gaelic sports experienced, his comments were also viewed as important for Irish Gaels in Scotland.

> It goes without saying that hurling, as we saw it, at Parkhead, is the king of the outdoor games, but I don't suppose it will ever make headway in a country given over to Association football.[44]

The G.A.A. in Scotland drew great store from the match. Although the Scottish representatives were beaten by a score of ten goals and five points to four goals and two points, the game was considered a 'decided success'. However, the Kilkenny men had shown the Scottish based players a lesson. Kilkenny were a fitter side and in fact the local G.A.A. considered the visitors champion sprinters as well as hurlers. W Dwyer of The Rapparees seemed the only player on the home side who had the capacity to match the visitors although the defence also received plaudits.

The Kilkenny Journal reported that five thousand spectators had attended the match, a figure which may have been an optimistic estimate. In a stadium which could reputedly hold eighty-two thousand people, even five thousand would not look substantial. The *Journal* spoke highly of the facilities at Celtic Park commenting that it was lamentable that they themselves did not have a similar structure at home.[45] At the post match celebrations, Mr O Toole, General Secretary of the G.A.A., announced that forthwith Scotland would become part of the new Provincial Council of Britain. This would mean that Scotland would now have to compete with the other counties of Britain, London, South Wales and Lancashire, to qualify for the All-Ireland championship.[46]

The game was viewed as having the potential to promote the sport amongst the Irish in Scotland but it met with competition on this occasion. On the same day at Whifflet in Coatbridge, the annual demonstration of Irish National Forresters took place, an organisation which had branches all over the west central belt and to which many Catholic families had at least one member attached. Many thousands of Irish Catholics attended this particular demonstration. While the Forresters, Hibernians and the Irish National League took up the political or welfare time of many Catholics in Scotland and Celtic Football Club dominated the sporting interests, 'native' Irish games suffered. Hurling and football continued in Scotland over the next few years but there seems to have been little resurgence as a direct result of the 'international' at Celtic Park. With the advent of 'the Great War' the following year, and the gradual unfolding of a pivotal stage in Irelands struggle against British rule, particularly with the 1916 Rising, the War of Independence and the Irish Civil War, the cultural and political landscape which the Irish in Scotland experienced was on the verge of cataclysmic change.

Notes

1. Purcell, 1982, p.70. Extract from letter to G.A.A. by the Fenian John O Leary after his release from exile in 1886.
2. Irish Post, 10/11/84, pp. 12–13.
3. Minutes of Central Council, 1900, pp. 31–32.
4. The Sam Maguire Cup, Cumann Luthchleas Gael, Dublin, 1986.
5. From John Denvir, The Irish in Britain, from the earliest times to the fall of Parnell, 1892, p. 447, quoted in Gallagher, 1987.
6. Glasgow Examiner, 20/4/1895.
7. Ibid: 24/8/1895.
8. Ibid: 11/9/1897.
9. Ibid: 30/1/1897.
10. Glasgow Observer, 14/6/1902.
11. Hugh McAleese died aged ninety in 1966.
12. Canning, 1979, originally from J E Handley, The Irish in Modern Scotland, Cork University Press, Cork, p. 233, 1947
13. Glasgow Examiner, 24/11/1900.
14. Feeney, 1995.
15. Glasgow Examiner, 15/6/1901.
16. Ibid: 23/5/1903.
17. Central Council Minutes, p. 149, 4/10/1903.
18. Glasgow Examiner, 13/6/1903.
19. Ibid: 4/7/1903.
20. Glasgow Star, 5/9/1903.
21. Feeney, 1995.
22. Ibid.

23. The Star, 6/5/1905.
24. Ibid: 15/7/1905.
25. Ibid: 5/3/1904.
26. Ibid: 4/2/1905.
27. Central Council minutes, May 1905.
28. McCourt probably originated from Dungannon, County Tyrone.
29. Gallagher, 1987, p. 97.
30. The Star, 18/4/1908.
31. Ibid: 18/8/1908. Patrick Costello, James Fynan and M Joyce were important activists in Dumbarton's hurling circles at this time.
32. The Star, 29/8/1908.
33. Irish Post, 10/11/1984.
34. Gaelsport G.A.A. Youth Annual, 1984.
35. The Star, 22/1/1909.
36. Ibid: 7/5/1909.
37. Ibid: 18/3/10.
38. Ibid: 8/3/1912.
39 Ibid: 22/3/1912.
40. Ibid: 13/9/1912.
41. Cork Free Press, 30/11/1912.
42. Irish Post, 17/11/1984.
43. The Star, 23/5/1913.
44. Ibid: 27/6/1913.
45. The Kilkenny Journal, 28/6/1913.
46. Glasgow Star, 27/6/1913.

CHAPTER 5
WAR AND CHANGE

Sinne Laochra Fáil, atá faoi gheall ag Éirinn
Buíon dár slua, thar toinn do tháinig chugainn:
Faoi mhóid bheith saor, seantir ár sinsear feasta
Ni fhágfar faoin tiorán ná faoin tráil,
Anocht a théam sa bhearna baoil
Le gean ar Ghaeil chun báis nó saoil
Le gunna-scréach, faoi lámhach na bpiléar
Seo libh, canaig' Amhrán na bhFiann[1]

Politics and culture

Among the Irish diaspora in Britain, many departed their adopted home to fight in the First World War. In the wake of the ending of the War, many subsequently decided to partake in Ireland's own struggle, the War of Independence. With the Great War, conscription and Ireland's struggle dominating the period, throughout Britain, Irish social and cultural organisations were detrimentally affected. In London, a 'golden era' of G.A.A. activities came to a close and this period witnessed the disbanding 'of club after club'.[2] Likewise, many non-Irish social organisations were also damaged by the convulsions caused by the War. For example, Scottish Shinty found itself ravaged by the effects of both the First and Second World Wars and, the subsequent economic and population dislocations, 'could have brought the [Shinty] Association to its knees'. Like many Irish organisations, shinty survived rather than thrived.[3]

During the War years the popular press in Britain was often dominated by reports of those killed in action in France or elsewhere. In Scotland, the columns of Irish and Catholic newspapers were full of names of young Catholic men, the vast majority either Irish born or of Irish forebears, also slain in the First World War. Inevitably many of the previously strong Irish organisations in the west central belt of Scotland were decimated as they lost large sections of their membership, and indeed, much of the next generation of leaders and organisers. Even when the war ended, with moral low and the unenviable depression of losing family and friends, some local organisations never regained their vibrancy.

With the political situation in Ireland having undergone much change since the beginning of the war, a new and more revolutionary impasse developed among the immigrant community. In areas of Lanarkshire and Glasgow, which had long been at the forefront of Irish politics and cultural activities, the 19th century cry of 'God Save Ireland' and 'A Nation Once Again' were replaced by the 'Soldiers Song': a song which by 1926 had become the Irish National Anthem. Members and associates of the G.A.A. were significantly involved in the 1916 Rising; Padraic Pearse, Sean McDermott, Con Colbert, Michael O'Hanrahan and Eamonn Ceannt, all leaders during the Rising, were executed in its wake. Others like Austin Stack and Michael Collins received prison services for their part in the insurrection. In Kerry, because of the involvement in Sinn Fein activities of so many of its members, the County Board found itself unable to field a team for the belated 1917 championship.[4]

In Scotland, as in Ireland, by 1919 the more revolutionary Sinn Fein Party began to replace the old Irish National League and other political bodies. Organisations such as the Hibernians also lost members though there was an overlap of membership with a number of these bodies. Nonetheless, the Irish political scene acquired a new vibrancy and meaning and many people's energies were devoted to political activities rather than cultural ones. From many of the areas were the G.A.A. were active emerged local Branches (Cumann) of Sinn Fein; in Motherwell (John O Leary Cumann), Port Glasgow and Greenock (Padraic Pearse Cumann), Glasgow (James Connolly Cumann), Clydebank (Joseph Plunkett Cumann), Hamilton (Patrick Pearse Cumann, Burnbank), Govan (Michael Mallin Cumann), Mossend (Padraic O Domnal Cumann — which had at least two hundred of a membership), Denny (Cormac Carrigan Cumann), Shotts (Sean MacDiarmada Cumann) and in Coatbridge there were at least three branches organised (Michael Mallin, Fr Griffen in the town's Whifflet area and Coatdyke's Thomas Ashe).

Even in popular Loyalist-Unionist strongholds such as Caldercruix and Larkhall in Lanarkshire, Sinn Fein Cumann also existed amongst the small Irish Catholic communities. It is estimated that the number of Sinn Fein branches in Scotland rose to around eighty fold during this period while the number of people who directly became involved in the developing Irish Republican Army was around three thousand in the Glasgow area alone.[5] Clearly the political situation in Ireland dominated within the Irish community in Scotland (indeed, it was a pre-eminent issue among the general population). So much so, that Eamon de Valera later revealed that the Irish in Scotland had contributed more money to the Republican struggle in Ireland than any other country, including Ireland itself.[6]

However, this period also marked the zenith of active nationalist support in Scotland. The years 1922–1923 saw the eruption of the fratricidal conflict of the Irish Civil War. Gallagher believes that the Irish in Scotland became confused and 'war wearied' as the fight in Ireland became less straightforward. Confusion over the situation in Ireland along with British anti-subversive actions also contributed to many in the immigrant community becoming less inclined in their political Irishness. Crucially for the Irish in Britain:

> the spectacle of Irishman killing Irishman greatly weakened Irish political and cultural movements in many British cities where these activities had reached a high pitch only a short time before.[7]

In Ireland, the effects of the Civil War in particular upon the youthful G.A.A. can be seen in County Clare where, until 1925, two rival County Boards were set up, one composed of pro-Treaty and the other of anti-Treaty gaels. As with even the most basic family unit, the G.A.A. experienced the Civil War from each perspective, having supporters on both sides of the divide.

Although in 1925 in Coatbridge Sinn Fein was instigating meetings in an attempt to revive the organisation,[8] the political parties which emerged in the new and independent 'Free State' of Ireland had a lesser need to create a British dimension than had their forbears in the Parliamentary Party and Sinn Fein. In Britain, the Labour Party and trade unions served as incorporatist agents by diverting the attentions of the Irish towards socio-political matters immediately relevant. The British state, its symbolism, ideas and identities forthwith acquired greater relevance for many Irish in Britain. Irish parties began to weaken in Britain as Ireland played a less significant part in the British political agenda. This meant that a new era of politics in the adopted home began to impinge upon many aspects of the immigrants and their offspring's lives. With the Irish Free State adjusting to its recently found independence, the new Northern Ireland state developed as a violent sectarian entity, largely hidden from the eyes of the public in Britain. As a result, Ireland's historical struggle declined in the immigrant mind. Although the Irish in Britain became involved in bodies such as the Anti-Partition League, Irish politics ceased to stir the same level of activity as in pre-partition days. Allied to this, immigration from Ireland to Scotland declined dramatically after the First World War and many of the Irish in Scotland began to acquire new party political allegiances which were the product of their everyday circumstances. Despite affinity with and loyalty to Ireland, many Irish recognised that they could be more influential in a local setting which after all, was the situation they found themselves and in which many of their aspirations were henceforth applicable. So began the Labour Party's deep reliance on the Irish in west-central Scotland: the main beneficiaries of Irish immigrants changing political experiences and perspectives.

Such experiences and perspectives also meant that the Irishness of the immigrant community was disadvantaged. The lessening role of Irish political activities combined with the growth of the immigrant community's ties with local politics through links with Labour Party, gradually supported a diminished attachment with their country of origin for many immigrants and their offspring. Although the immigrants maintained their links to Ireland in a variety of ways, this period marks a watershed for the kind of unity that had previously existed. More significantly, this was also a time when being viewed as Irish was particularly difficult in a society which contained important elements overtly hostile to the presence of Irish Catholics in Scotland.[9] Although this experience negatively affected the Irishness of the immigrant community, by the end of the 20th century Irish identity still remained a notable factor in the social, cultural and political composition of the Catholic community in Scotland.

The experiences of War and subsequent social and political changes in Britain, especially the growing demands of the working classes, transformed the context of social, cultural and political lifestyles. The developing political system, the advent of progressive educational change and the growth of the mass media meant that common cultural pastimes and traits developed as never before. These factors drew people towards actual and perceived shared public experiences which in turn helped produce conventional and popular factors and features of identity. In turn, these began to have a significant impact on the solidarity and communal nature, as well as the self-image, of the Irish in Scotland. Such alterations invariably introduced a challenge to existing identities, especially those which had a strong grounding in religious beliefs and attitudes.

Notes

1. Amhran na Bhfiann (Irish National Anthem)
2. Irish Post, 17/11/1984.
3. Sport of the Gael (Shinty), BBC Scotland (television), 1993.
4. de Burca, 1980, p. 139.
5. Gallagher, 1987, p. 90.
6. O Connor, 1970, pp. 141–142.
7 Gallagher, 1987, pp. 94–97.
8. The Star, 9/1/1925.
9. See chapter 5.

CHAPTER 6

IDENTITY IN FLUX

This would be grand if only every Irishman would kill a negro, and be hanged for it. I find this sentiment generally approved — sometimes with the qualification that they want Irish and negroes for servants, not being able to get any other.[1]

The Post-War Irish

Like many social and cultural activities, gaelic sports in Scotland were depleted by the effects of the First World War, as well as the Irish War of Independence in its aftermath. Many thousands of Irishmen, including second and third generation immigrants to Scotland, lost their lives in the Great War. Amongst the motives for taking part; for some it was their employment to be part the army, some fought as much against a common enemy as for Britain, whilst for others it was regarded as a stepping stone towards some form of Irish independence. During this time, the Labour Movement and the cause of the working man gained prominence amongst the working-classes, and related activities began to dominate the non-working time of many of those hitherto without a political voice.

As 'agents of change', the Great War, War in Ireland, as well as the increasing salience of Labour activity, all marked a watershed in Irish activities in Scotland. In the years before the War the Irish Catholic press contained numerous adverts and reports on Irish activities; the Irish National League, the Irish National Forresters, the Irish Independent League, the Ancient Order of Hibernians, Sinn Fein Cumann, the Gaelic League, the Irish Literary Association and an array of county and provincial associations, including Tyrone, Monaghan, Armagh, Cavan and Derry in particular, Connacht and Leinster, as well as a number of sporting bodies from athletics to swimming clubs. In addition, a variety of Catholic associations like the League of the Cross, the Catholic Men's Society and the Catholic Truth Society were active organisations among the immigrant community. The most significant facet of Irishness and indeed cultural Catholicism for

46

the rest of the twentieth century also prevailed: Celtic Football and Athletic Club. Nonetheless, for most of these bodies, decline in the face of secularisation and a new cultural and political context ensued.

Little gaelic sporting activity is apparent during these years. Certainly some clubs were playing the occasional game such as a Pearse Harps — Patrick Sarsfields football match during 1920,[2] as well as the founding of another hurling club in Coatbridge in the same year.[3] However, there were few official organised football or hurling games taking place. By the end of 1921 an attempt was made to reinvigorate the gaelic sporting scene. The Association in Scotland was re-organised and twelve clubs were represented at the first meeting held in Glasgow chaired by Maurice Frieze. Frieze, who lived in Rutherglen, Glasgow, was arrested two years later when British police swooped on thirty-eight suspected prominent republicans in Scotland and seventy-two in England. With the assistance of the new pro-treaty Free State government, the suspects were deported to Ireland where they were imprisoned in Mountjoy Gaol, Dublin.[4] By the end of the Civil War they had been released. The following year the deportees from Scotland received £17,000 in compensation for the unwieldy way they had they had been dealt with.[5] Distinct from the politics of some of its membership, the noted Glasgow G.A.A. meeting was also important for the presence of two women, Misses Mullen and McKenna representing the Glasgow Camogie Club.[6] Subsequently, 1922 marked the first time gaelic sports became manifest among the women of the immigrant community. Under the auspices of the Camoguidneacht Association at least one camogie match took place the following year, between Granuailes of Glasgow and Taras of Gourock. The teams which participated in that match were:

Granuailes: J Donnellan, T MacBride, J McGranahan, L Gallagher, M McGowan, M O Connor, L Canney, L McLeod, A O Reilly, B Gormley, M B Marr and B Lynch.

Taras: G McDonald, M Flavin, R Kelly, Butson, Dorrien, Brennen, McElhinney, Healy, McKenna, Morrisay, Foley and Doyle.

By 1922, football and hurling began to played more regularly and teams in both Glasgow and Lanarkshire areas temporarily found a new lease of life. Along with some of the established clubs in Glasgow and Lanarkshire, others clubs began in Hamilton

(Emmets), Springburn (McCurtains Gaels), Kinning Park (O Tooles), whilst gaels in Dumbarton responded with two clubs, Dr Crokes and Cuchulains.

A degree of 'Celtic spirit' was reflected among Irish and Scottish highland gaels when in 1922 a select hurling team from Glasgow played the Skye Shinty Club in a compromise game. Although the hurlers won the first half of the match under the rules of the G.A.A., the game was won by the Skye Club with a final score of five goals and one point to three goals.[7] The Skye representatives were additionally asked to attend the proposed 1922 Tailteann Games in Ireland, a national festival of athletics, art, music and poetry. These games were intended to revive a tradition going back to the 7th century when they were originally instituted in memory of Queen Tailte. The first games hosted competitors from Ireland's four provinces and had survived uninterrupted until 1169 when Ireland was invaded from its neighbouring island.

As a result of problems relating to finance and the eruption of the Irish Civil War, as well as the general disruption caused by conflict within and between various areas of the country, in Ireland, the development of the G.A.A. was to encounter another term of struggle. The proposed games of 1922 did not take place. As a result of the Civil War, most G.A.A. activities in Munster and Connacht came to a halt whilst Ulster continued to labour amidst its own particular circumstances. Only in Leinster were fixtures fulfilled, notably for the first time since 1916.[8] Nevertheless, the Association in Ireland avoided the serious political fission which might have crippled it.

Until the founding of the Irish Free State, athletics in Ireland were under the control of the G.A.A.. However, until 1924 Irish athletes had to compete for Britain or else emigrate and adopt the colours of another country. Protests to the International Amateur Athletic Federation by British representatives also persuaded that body only to accept athletes from the Free State, viewing athletes from the North as being from a different country. This went against the hitherto united Irish effort involving athletes from the whole island and the subsequent confusion and division split athletics in the Free State for many decades. As a manifestation of these troubles, after many years of promise the Tailteann Games, involving sporting and cultural events, were eventually held in 1924. These games intended to stress the independent sporting

48

strong
link
between
GAA +
Athletics

IDENTITY IN FLUX

and cultural nature of the Irish people and were sponsored by the new Irish Government rather than the G.A.A, although the Association did provide many of its leading officials as well as the main stadium. Joining the Irish on this occasion was a team of shinty players from Scotland. An early shock to the festival hosts came when a Scottish shinty team beat an Irish hurling side two to one. However, by the time the hurling tournament got underway, the Irish hurlers clearly regained their self-respect. The tournament produced the following scores:

Table 6.1
Tailteann Games 1924: Gaelic football and Hurling/Shinty scores

Ireland	4:3	America	1:3
America	4:2	England	3:2
Scotland	7:3	Wales	5:1
Ireland	5:4	Wales	2:6
Ireland	9:3	England	4:7
Wales	6:2	England	5:3
America	6:6	Scotland	2:3
Ireland	10:1	Scotland	4:5
Ireland	4:6	America	3:2 (final)

The team which originated in Scotland was led by James J Jackson, whose parents were from County Monaghan. In later years, Jackson was also to become one of the founders of the Irish National Association in Scotland.

One game of gaelic football was held at the games when the home side beat the English representatives 3:9 to 2:3. Although such matches made the games seem quite international, it appears that the British sides were in fact represented by Irish based sportsmen. Purcell comments on how many Irish viewed the games:

> the contingents of exiles from the United States, Canada, Britain, New Zealand, Australia and South Africa gave our people a sense of pride in realising how our small island had contributed to the building of other and more powerful nations in every quarter of the globe.[9]

Irish had
strong
influence
a large
nations

Despite thousands of people attending, the games they were not regarded as an unqualified success. *The Glasgow Star and Examiner* condemned the expense being laid out whilst Sinn Fein and other groups boycotted the games in protest at the

unrest

after
war

imprisoning of republicans.[10] Nine days before the games commenced, the Free State Government released the last of these prisoners, including Eamon de Valera, Austin Stack and Sean McCarthy. However, the boycott remained. Although the Tailteann games, revived after a lapse of seven and a half centuries, and were held again in 1928 and in 1932, they were not on the same scale as the earlier event and there was no football or hurling representatives from Britain. The games failed in their aim of reflecting pride in the antiquity, survival and identity of the Irish people. Aside from a few positive signs of gaelic sporting activity, and although Central Council in Dublin sent Mr McGrath to Britain to re-organise the sport, little more was heard of hurling, gaelic football or camogie in Scotland for a number of years. Notably missing since 1914, it was 1927 before Britain returned to compete in All-Ireland championships, having the status of junior footballers and hurlers.

The slowing down of Irish immigration to Scotland after the First World War undoubtedly had a cultural impact upon some facets of Irish identity. Census figures showed that the Irish-born population of Scotland had declined from its peak of 218,745 in 1881, to just over 200,000 at the turn of the century and to 159,020 by 1921. Moreover, by this time, 88,397 had been born in the area of Northern Ireland and 70,623 born in the new Irish Free State. With the G.A.A. taking until the 1930s before making a significant impact upon much of Ulster many Irish immigrants to Scotland had in fact little native grounding in gaelic sport. In addition, many immigrants were women who had employment and familial priorities as opposed to the sporting and cultural ones sometimes displayed by male members of the diaspora.

All Jock Tamson's Bairns?

With the Irish political scene undergoing profound change, and in view of the immigrants' response to these changes, as well as their new found political circumstances in Scotland, traditional identities became a more complex feature of society. The immigrant community experienced circumstances which lent towards a dilution of the strength of their Irishness. To date, many people from that community had recognised their Irish ethnic and national identity and from where in Ireland they originated. However, the coherence or harmony within Irish identity began

THE LEAGUE CHAMPIONSHIP.

Apes and Aryans. *Scottish Referee*, 3 February 1905

6. A common view of the Irish in early 20th-century Scotland.

to be affected in a way hitherto not experienced to such a significant extent.

Anti-Irish and anti-Catholic feeling in Scotland is partly documented by some social scientists.[11] However, it has rarely been a phenomenon characterised by uniformity. It is complex, differing from individual to individual, from organisation to organisation, and from community to community. Also, for many Scots, it has no part to play in their lives. Nonetheless, the history of ethno-religious cleavage in Scotland has meant that opposition and prejudice towards the immigrant community has traditionally been widespread and has clearly had wide resonance in Scotland. During the inter war period it was a particularly popular manifestation within Scottish society.

Cooney asserts that as late as 1938, the Church and Nation Committee of the Church of Scotland emphasised: 'the elementary right of a nation to control and select its immigrants'.[12] The debate which had resulted in such a way of thinking was conducted solely with Irish Catholics in mind. Brown, states that from around the time of the Education Act (Scotland) 1918, until the outbreak of the Second World War, there was an 'official' Presbyterian campaign against the Irish Catholic community in Scotland.[13] This campaign was both institutional and popular, and is viewed by Brown as an attempt at 'marginalising, and even eliminating an ethnic minority whose presence was regarded as an evil, polluting the purity of Scottish race and culture'.[14]

This period was a fertile one for such activities as well as a time when they were acceptable to and supported by many people in the wider society. Such sentiments found expression in popular literature, for example in the works of Andrew Dewar Gibb (later to become Regius Professor of Scots Law at Glasgow University) and of journalist George Malcolm Thomson.[15] Political activists, like Alexander Ratcliffe and John McCormick, gained success at the ballot by declaring similar anti-Irish and anti-Catholic opinions. Other significant political figures at the time reflected these widespread feelings regarding the Irish in Scotland. Conservative member of Parliament, Lord Scone, believed that:

> culturally the Irish population...has not been assimilated into the Scottish population. It is not my purpose to discuss now whether the Irish culture is good or bad, but merely to state the definite fact that there is in the west of Scotland a completely separate race of alien origin practically homogeneous whose presence there is bitterly resented by tens of thousands of the Scottish working-class.[16]

As persons born in England but living in Scotland outnumbered those who were Irish born in Scotland, such attitudes towards the Irish were conceived within a context of Britain's historic relationship with the island of Ireland as well as by the well established anti-Catholicism which dominated or filtered through many areas of Scottish society.

The contrary influences of the First World War experience and the resultant loss of a great deal of Irish cultural and national vibrancy clearly affected the Irish in Scotland. The negative effects upon the Irish diaspora of the conflict in Ireland, the incorporatist influences of Catholic education, largely controlled by the British state,[17] the positive opening up of British society in a social and political sense and the development of the common cultural features and experiences of the 20th century, all had an effect upon the Irishness of the immigrant community. Significantly, so also did the racial hostility and religious sectarianism encountered by the Irish and which marked that community's experience in Scotland. Although this encounter was complex and multi-varied, and despite a number of Scots making no contribution to it, antagonism characterised many individual and popular perceptions.[18]

The anti-Catholic and anti-Irish nature of significant areas of life during the 1920s and 1930s made a critical impression upon the self perceptions and images of the immigrant diaspora in Scotland. Irishness remained important to many within the community, as is reflected in the strength of Irish identity in the late 20th century. However, this period helped create one of the strategies constructed by the Irish to contend with adversity in Scotland. Thus, becoming less obviously Irish was an important part of a strategy which many consciously or unconsciously embarked upon. After all, if such campaigns against the Irish in Scotland had met with more obvious success, the result might have been deportation. In the context of such negative portrayals, it seems an obvious question to ask, who in society wished to be associated with Ireland or the Irish? For others who were anti-Irish, a less distinctive Irish identity and community within Scottish society might not have dampened some of their antagonism, but it may have relieved its worst features. If the Irish were here to stay and could not be viably rejected, then rather than negatively affect a perceived purity in the Scottishness of the host community, the Irish would have to be assimilated. Irishness remained largely unacceptable, but the Irish might be more acceptable if they became more Scottish.

Partly as a response to the ethno-religious circumstances the diaspora experienced in Scotland, from the 1930s Catholic identity, in relation to a diminishing Irishness, became the predominant feature of the immigrant community. A change amongst the Irish which manifested itself in a less visible Irish identity, is reflected in an increasing Catholic emphasis in the Irish political, cultural and religious organ, *The Glasgow Star and Examiner.* Irish politics and cultural activities continued to be reported in Catholic newspapers but as they receded in prominence, they did so at the expense of purely Catholic or religious matters. Sport in general and even news relating to Celtic Football Club in particular also suffered in this newspaper. Newspapers such as *The Glasgow Star* became less partisan and engaged in a struggle to be viewed as impartial in things Irish and political: more often than not, ignoring Irish and political affairs altogether. A product of this process was the gradual diminishing of news in relation to Ireland and the Irish in Scotland. *'The Star'* was one newspaper which began a trend amongst Catholic newspapers in Scotland reflecting a gradual shift towards reporting articles Scottish rather than matters Irish as was previously the case.

Up until this time standard reporting, reflecting the Irish background and origins of the mass of these newspapers Catholic readership, was replaced by a portrayal of things considered pre-Reformation Scottish Catholic. Articles such as 'Catholic Scotland', 'How the Highland's held the faith' and 'Scotland's martyrs' began to predominate, stories important to the history of Scotland, but of limited relevance to the history of the Irish in Scotland.[19] Finally, with the death in 1934 of Derryman Charles Diamond, owner of much of the Catholic and Irish press in Britain, a new era for Irish ethnic newspapers dawned. By 1935, *The Glasgow Star* announced its forthwith 'strictly non-political' position whilst its 'aims and ideals [were subsequently] devoted entirely to the Catholic cause'.[20]

Henceforth, along with the absence of any positive mention of Ireland in state Catholic schools' curriculum, the cultural conformity engendered by the growing mass media (including the lack of reporting on matters Irish), Irishness and links with Ireland became for some of the diaspora, secondary, subordinate and less familiar. In many ways, Ireland and being Irish became less accessible. In addition, for some of the Irish community in Scotland, to be viewed as Scottish was a mark of success. For some immigrants, Ireland represented the poverty and oppression of the past. A perception existed that to be seen as Irish was to be viewed as parochial, ignorant and permanently ghettoised.[21] The less visible Irishness amongst Irish immigrants in Scotland and the steady adoption of a new framework of identity for some immigrants, has since characterised many of the offspring of the Irish. Antagonism and hostility on the part of a variety of institutions, organisations and individuals throughout Scottish society, helped create and sustain an atmosphere where to be seen as Irish meant that life chances were perceived as being limited. Almost inevitably, part of the Irish Catholic response to this hostility was a privatisation as well as dilution of Irish identity.

The emerging Catholic identity, which began to dominate the traditional Irish Catholic one in west central Scotland, consisted of strong assimilationist obligations. These obligations operated on the assumption that everyone in Scotland and even Britain shared significant social and political features. For some commentators like Hickman, such a promotion was part of a conscious strategy to diminish the Irishness of this community: the Irish in Britain were being incorporated into the British State and in the process Irishness was replaced with British and Scottish identities.[22] The traditional view of the Irish being different in religion, culture and politics, of being a community which in times of trouble in Ireland provided authorities in Britain with a perceptible element of threat, was partly changed by this strategy of assimilation. A speech by Archbishop Hindley in England summed up the growing dominance of Scottish and British cultural attributes over those which were arguably of greater significance to the immigrants:

> Such loyalty to God and our Sovereign, George VI, who has succeeded to the dignity and to the heavy responsibility which were laid down by his brother. In unswerving sincerity the 17,000,000 of, Catholics throughout the Empire do homage to our new King, and declare their devotion to his person and their attachment to the royal family...[23]

Hindley's comments parallel those of the Scottish Bishop Hay in the late 18th century. Although in an era of pre-Irish immigration Catholic Scots at that time remained an object for hostility. The dominant Protestant identities of the Scottish people encouraged the remaining Catholic population in the country to maintain a low profile. This low profile, and indeed the subservient nature of contemporary Catholicism, was evident during the period of the passing of Catholic relief bills in 1788. Throughout this time of crisis, Bishop George Hay protested that Scots Catholics were innocent and loyal, thus emphasising the abstruse and servile nature of the native Scottish Catholic church.[24] Such comments pre-dated, but also anticipated an era in the 20th century when the Catholic Irish became a focus for hostility. A frequent response from that community towards this enmity resembled that of Scottish Catholics in the late 18th century. The Irish also maintained a low profile amid a social and political hostility which targeted them and helped create a climate where expressions of Irishness were likely to attract unwanted antagonism.

Notes

1. Curtis 1988.
2. The Star, 28/2/1920.
3. Ibid: 17/7/1920.
4. Ibid: 17/3/1923.
5. Gallagher, 1987, p. 97.
6. The Star, 17/12/1921.
7. The Star, 15/7/1922.
8. de Burca, 1980, p. 161.
9. Purcell, 1982, p. 192.
10. The Star, 30/8/1924.
11. See Devine, McFarland, Gallagher.
12. Cooney, 1982, p. 19.
13. Brown, 1991, pp. 19–45.
14. Ibid: p. 21.
15. Gallagher, 1987, p. 168–172.
16. Hansard, 261, 22/11/1932.
17. Hickman, 1995.
18. See Bradley, 1995.
19. For examples see The Star, 11/1/1936, 12/12/1936 and 1/2/1936.
20. The Star, 7/9/1935.
21. Gallagher's excellent biographical work 'Glasgow: The Uneasy Peace', also reflects the non-specific sub-theme of an Irish ghetto population in the West of Scotland.
22. Hickman, 1995.
23. The Star, 26/12/1936.
24. Cooney, 1982, p. 14.

CHAPTER 7

GAELIC SPORT IN SCOTLAND

The Association...shall foster an awareness and love of the national ideals in the people of Ireland, and assist in promoting a community spirit through its clubs.[1]

Struggle for Survival

By the 1930s the Gaelic Athletic Association in Scotland was facing its lowest ebb. It had long since struggled to be recognised even amongst its own community in Scotland but with the changing social, cultural and political environment within which it existed, its chances for survival were severely restricted.

In July 1932 a letter from 'Old Faugh' in *The Glasgow Star and Examiner* confirmed a lack of gaelic sporting activity in the west of Scotland:

Is there such a thing in Glasgow or district as a hurling club or Irish Athletic Club...I used to play myself on ground in Possilpark, now used for a housing scheme. And I am sure there are a lot of people in Glasgow who if they had the chance would be only too pleased to join up in such a club...[2]

The question was to be partly answered by Thomas Flynn, Sports Convenor of the Irish National Association based at 64 Charlotte Street in Glasgow (later based at Risk Street off London Road in the east of the city). Along with James Jackson, the Irish National Association was founded by Con Horgan from Cork, Willie Farrell and Richard Ford. Ford was an Irish and Catholic activist who had been president of the first branch of the Gaelic League to be founded in Scotland and was later prominent in the Catholic Knights of St Columba. It was as president of the Irish National Association, that Ford, a former player with the Rapparees and over the previous twenty or so years renowned amongst the gaelic fraternity for his lectures on 'Poetical Wild Flowers',[3] stated:

The Irish National Association since its inception has used every means in its power to foster a love for the Irish arts and games among the young Irishmen and women in Glasgow. During the past session

57

we have been amply repaid in the dancing and musical sections as the results of the recent Sinn Fein Feis in Glasgow show. We have recently acquired a commodious sports ground of six and a quarter acres at Marylea [adjacent to the Franciscan Convent]...We have a hurling field in the grounds and have started a hurling club. In passing I may mention that we have also a County Board of the G.A.A...[4]

A hurling club was indeed started by the early months of the following year, but the truth was that the Gaelic Athletic Association was not flowering in Scotland.[5]

In early 1933, after initial contacts between representatives of the Irish National Association and the Southern Shinty League, an advertisement in the *Glasgow Observer* appealed for support for a new initiative:

that the Irish people in Glasgow will give them the support it would receive in Ireland by turning out in large numbers to give the Irish team a hearty welcome and show that the exiles still hold dear the National games of Ireland.[6]

The result of the meeting was the arrangement of a fixture between a Irish university hurling team playing a compromise rules game against a selection of players from the Scottish Shinty League at Shieldhall Park, Hardgate Road, south Govan in Glasgow. The hurling team was composed of players from the University colleges of Dublin, Cork and Galway. The Glasgow Southern Shinty League selection were all of Highland birth and descent. The hurlers won the match by the only goal of the game.[7] Nonetheless, according to one report:

the result was of secondary importance to the fact that this essentially Gaelic game was shown to have a large following in the West of Scotland and the possibilities for its development are attractive.[8]

In terms of the match itself, it was reported that:

Our Irish visitors put more play on the ball, changed and interchanged positions with fine understanding, made ground more quickly and the harassed Scots had to reveal to the full their renowned characteristics — doggedness and tenacity — to withstand periods of uninterrupted attacks. J Canning, one of Erin's priest forwards, scored the goal after 18 minutes play, netting from short range...The second half was more evenly contested: indeed at times the speed of the play exhilarated.[9]

The G.A.A. in Scotland looked anxiously for revival. In October of the same year, Rev Daniel O Keeffe of St Charles Kelvinside, Glasgow, Rev Daniel Horgan, the Irish National Association, acting as an intermediary for the G.A.A. in Dublin, along with Mr P O Keeffe, Secretary of the G.A.A. in Ireland and Mr P McNamee, secretary of the Ulster Council, met with officials of the Camanachd Association in Scotland: 'with a view to unifying the rules of hurling and shinty'.[10] Among the Camanachd representatives were ex-provost Skinner from Oban and Messrs Fletcher (Glasgow) and Patterson (Beauly). The result of the meeting was that future games between hurling and shinty representatives would be directed by the attending members at this meeting: they would 'settle points of divergence in the unified game'.[11] Nonetheless, the Camanachd Association officials subsequently decided not to compromise on their rules for games in Scotland although some accommodation might be made for future international games. Hutchinson states that government officials in Edinburgh and Whitehall learned of the contact between both Associations and made representations to the Camanachd body stressing the 'anti-British political flavour' of the G.A.A. For Hutchinson, it was the shinty players of Scotland who lost out. The refusal to understand the G.A.A.s origins and evolution as part of the struggle for Irish independence, and the willingness to accept government views meant:

> self-imposed solitude in the country to which the Irish had introduced it [shinty] 1500 years before.[12]

Irish feelings were more positive on Irish-Scottish matters. At the annual meeting of the Gaelic Athletic Association's Ard Comairle held in Thurles County Tipperary in the following year, the Council claimed that:

> The position in Scotland, so long uncertain, has been transformed during the past year by special re-organisation and an understanding with the Camanacht Association in the Western area.[13]

Despite plans and expectations, nothing appears to have been done during the rest of the year. At a variety of junctures during the 20th century some efforts were made to substantiate competition between hurlers in Ireland and shinty players in Scotland: this was especially true between some Irish and Scottish university sides. However, the Scottish shinty authorities did not welcome the Irish competition and in 1964 the Camanachd Association went so far as to pronounce itself to be 'firmly against any links' with gaelic sports in Ireland, requesting its members not to patronise any compromise game which might be organised. In 1971, Blessed Oliver Plunkett School from Dublin travelled to play Oban High School. Hutchinson believes that this event meant that, 'the ice was broken'. Since then, clubs in both countries have played each other and a number of 'international' matches have also been held.[14]

In 1934 the Gaelic Athletic Association celebrated its Jubilee: fifty years as a major institution in Ireland. The newspaper of the Catholic Irish in Scotland, *The Glasgow Star*, was moved to comment:

> ...the G.A.A. is the healthiest lay movement we have in Ireland and is the one continuous platform for unity of action that nationalists have developed. The controlling body of the Association have brought it safely through the dark and dreary days of external and internal trouble, and their outspoken loyalty to the Faith of their Fathers is all the guarantee we need that in piloting it successfully through the political shoals of today.[15]

Another attempt was made to revive the games the same year and a hurling match at the Clontarf Park grounds in Marylea was arranged as an opener to the revival. During August, Rovers from Cambuslang met the Fitzgeralds of Glasgow with the former winning by three goals and two points to one goal and three points. The match was refereed by Rev Daniel O Keeffe. Pater, Dwyer, McCallion and Haugh scored for the Rovers whilst M J McCann and Sugrve replied for the Fitzgeralds.

> A most encouraging feature of the game was the good play shown by the neophytes under the skilled guidance of veterans of national reputation in Ireland. Among them were former heroes of hurling of Glens of Antrim, Tipperary, Clare, Limerick, Sligo and Cork. The Scottish Provincial Council has started well...[16]

Despite some optimism, it was August 1934 before the revival was again reflected in press reports. A meeting on the part of the Clontarf Park Committee believed that:

for the development of Gaelic games and outdoor amusements...an optimistic feeling prevailed. Sincere thanks (were) accorded to many patrons for their generous donations and through the gift of 7 sets of hurleys from the National Council, G.A.A., Dublin a promising future is believed to be secure.

Having turned with jealous eyes to the flourishing condition of Gaelic games in London and America, the apathy still prevailing in Scotland was deprecated. The important bearing of our games on national character of which we are so justly proud, cannot be exaggerated. The idea of a national recreation ground where the people throughout the city (Glasgow) are drawn together...cannot be sufficiently stressed...

Gaelic pastimes as an aspect of guarding against the excesses of industrialisation and urbanisation, and the cultural and national security afforded by the Association in an often hostile land, recreated some of the ideals of the original founders of the G.A.A. for this writer at least. He continued:

How the glad thoughts of happy associations in Clontarf Park where all hearts beat in unison in the friendly Celtic way, where friends meet friend once more — all for each and each for all — can enliven many a weary hour in the office, the salesroom or the factory or lost amidst the mass of swarming humanity. Remember that procrastination is the thief of time, an earnest appeal is made to the youthful exiles — boys and girls — scattered throughout the city to take immediate advantage of the long-looked-for opportunity and to assist the good work already begun under their patronage and memberships.[17]

Yet despite the existence of committed gaelic enthusiasts and continued attempts on the part of the Irish National Association, who were at the forefront of gaelic Irish activities, to revive gaelic games and other Irish pursuits and pastimes, few successes resulted. Probably the last reference made to gaelic games played in Scotland for a number of years is found in the Glasgow Observer of October 1934.[18] A hurling match was arranged between sides from Glasgow and Lanarkshire. Played at Lanarkshire Park in Motherwell, the Glasgow team won the game with six goals and two points against five goals and two points. The teams which took the field were:

Glasgow: Dwyer, Lillies, Howe, McCallum, Ahern, Gallagher, Burns, Martin, Butler, Gillian, H Dolan, Walsh, Hughes and McCarran.

Lanarkshire: T Kiernan, Myles, H McCann, M McCann, McAlinden, D Dickson, Lambert, O Connor, H Kiernan, Boylan, Devlin and Sugrve.[19]

This game in Lanarkshire was probably the last competitive hurling match to be organised in Scotland for a number of years. Canning believes that World War II decimated the G.A.A. as it did many other organisations.

Hurling, whatever about Gaelic football, virtually disappeared from the Scottish scene. Fortunately due to bettering conditions in Ireland, the influx of Irish to Scotland had dried up to a mere trickle and consequently the youth and material of the G.A.A. games simply did not exist.[20]

Irishness was still important within the Catholic community in Scotland, as partly reflected in the thousands who followed Celtic Football Club and the 40,000 who turned out for a demonstration by the Ancient Order of Hibernians at Carfin in Lanarkshire in August 1937: but gaelic sports struggled to rise above the status of a 'minority sport'.[21] Few families who were Irish, Irish minded or of Irish antecedents, had any affinity for these uniquely Irish sports. By the 1940s popular and public Irish cultural activities, and gaelic sports in particular, were at a low ebb in the west of Scotland. It was some years before gaelic enthusiasts recognised that for Irish sporting activities to survive and become popular, a concerted effort was required to recruit young people of Irish antecedents. Indeed, gaelic activity, as a facet of being Irish in Scotland, would virtually require to be introduced as a new sport to many of those with Irish forebears. Nonetheless, in the immediate years after the Second World War, a revival in Scotland did take place, 'chiefly attributable to the post World War II situation when Irish immigrants found great demand for their labour in the vast building and construction developments' then underway.[22]

Notes

1. G.A.A. Constitution and Rules, 4a.
2. The Star, 20/8/1932.
3. Ibid: 20/9/1912.
4. Ibid: 27/8/1932.
5. Ibid: 14/4/1934.
6. Glasgow G.A.A. Centenary Brochure, 1984.
7. The Star, 13/5/1933.
8. Glasgow G.A.A. Centenary Brochure, 1984.
9. Ibid
10. The Star, 9/9/1933.
11. Ibid: 21/10/1933.
12. Hutchinson 1989, pp. 186–187.
13. Minutes of Central Council, 1934.
14. Hutchinson, 1989, pp. 186–187.
15. The Star, 22/9/1934.
16. Glasgow G.A.A. Centenary Brochure, 1984.
17. Ibid
18. This match was played on 29th of September.
19. Boylan was probably Michael Boylan who originated from Ballina, County Mayo. A number of this family are believed to have subsequently emigrated from Motherwell to the Pittsburgh Steelworks in the U.S.A. From interview with member of Boylan family in Motherwell.
20. Glasgow G.A.A. Centenary Brochure, 1984.
21. The Star, 28/8/1937.
22. Michael Fallon in Glasgow G.A.A. Centenary Brochure, 1984.

CHAPTER 8

REGENERATION

All manner of leisure pursuits, and sport in particular, have played an important role in affirmations of identity and unity.[1]

Survival: Return to Gaelic Sport

For most of the 1930s gaelic sporting activities in Scotland existed in a state of flux, much of the period characterised by little if any Irish sports. In fact, it was the late 1940s before G.A.A. activities began to re-emerge in west central Scotland. After a few long term visits prior to the Second World War, aged twenty-five, John Keaveny finally immigrated to Glasgow in 1943. A native of County Sligo, Keaveny began to socialise with others in Glasgow who originated from Ireland. This occurred mainly at the numerous ceilis then being held around the Glasgow area, many taking place in venues such as the A.O.H. Hall in Greenvale Street Bridgeton, as well as in the Fianna Fail Club in Clyde Ferry Street, Glasgow.

Along with several other gaels, Keaveny took over the running of G.A.A. affairs in Glasgow from earlier Association figures such as Tom Flynn and Tom Gillespie. The Gillespie family were well known Donegal republicans from Buncrana, whose members had participated in the struggle for Irish independence in the first quarter of the 20th century. Gillespie, and subsequently his son Dermot, encouraged others such as Rory Campbell to become involved in G.A.A. affairs.[2] Campbell's people had came to Scotland from County Tyrone and his father too had previously been involved in republican activities in the period prior to the onset of the Second World War.[3]

Keaveny, previously a gaelic footballer in his native Geevagh, County Sligo, settled in East Kilbride during the mass re-locations of much of Glasgow's population to Scotland's 'New Towns' during the 1950s and 1960s. Along with Owen Kelly, Rory Campbell and Charlie Quinn, the latter having immigrated from Dromore, County Tyrone in the 1940s, he was instrumental in the re-forming of the Glasgow G.A.A.: the formal inauguration taking place at the Diocesan Centre near Charing Cross in Glasgow.[4] Keaveny was also one of the first individuals to begin to encourage the game amongst those of Irish descent in the west of Scotland. This reflected in the Thomas Davis Club from Motherwell which chiefly comprised players born in Scotland of an Irish background. These included Frank McIlheney and Gerry Gallen, the latter also a member of the Gaelic League. Gallen's father immigrated from Donegal, his mother from Tyrone while his wife originated from County Leitrim.[5]

In Lanarkshire, matches were played at Carfin's Glenburn Stadium, owned by the Heffernan family, and until the late 1990s, still being used as a dog racing track. Pat Heffernan, son of the original owner, was also a player with the Thomas Davis Club while matches were played at this venue during the late 1940s and early 1950s. Heffernan's mother came to Scotland from Cavan whilst his fathers side were earlier immigrants from west Munster. South east of Glasgow, Orion Park in Carmyle became the ground of another new club, Tara Harps, based originally at the Irish Club in Greenvale Street, Bridgeton in Glasgow. Formally the A.O.H. Hall this subsequently became the Tara Social Club.

However, the first Gaelic Football Club to emerge after the war took place when a few members of the Gaelic League, overlapping their membership with that of the Four Provinces Social Club in Paisley, began a fund raising venture mainly in the form of weekly ceilis, to finance the founding of a gaelic football club. On raising the sum of £100 the membership decided to purchase a football strip for the proposed Paisley Gaels Club, later to be known as Clan na Gael. The Club was born due in the main to the efforts of Father James Nevin from the local St Mirrin's Parish, Plunkett Cairns, Packy McCusker, Owen Kelly, Seamus McManus and Frank McCarron.

Over the last few years of the 1940s Paisley Gaels, in addition to several other gaelic participants, began to play gaelic football on an ash pitch near St Agnes' Church in Lambhill, Glasgow: this, courtesy of local priest, James Fennessy. Playing on ash meant that improved playing conditions became a priority for some members of the local G.A.A. Although hurling had dominated amongst the gaelic fraternity during the first fifty years of Irish gaelic sports in Scotland, it was gaelic football (arguably stylistically nearer the more dominant anglicised soccer and rugby games) which would provide the Association in Scotland with its future.

From the Gorbals area of Glasgow subsequently originated the Eire Og Club, mainly consisting of recent immigrants from the Rosses and Gweedore areas of Donegal.[6] The Round Towers club also emerged as did St Eunans based in Clydebank. The Padraic Pearses club had its base in the Fianna Fail Cumann's Club in Glasgow's Rutherglen Road, the only branch of Fianna Fail to be founded outside of Ireland. Most of the players playing with the club were originally from the Donegal gaeltacht, although some team members were second generation Irish.[7] A team also emerged from within the Irish community in Edinburgh, organised by John Doran and situated within St Mary's Cathedral Parish in the city.

In 1952 Pearses won the Glasgow Football Championship, celebrating with a visit and game against Cavan county champions, Baillieborough. During this time gaelic games in Scotland were regarded as being of a high standard. The Pearse team which played in Ireland was:

> P Comiskey, P O'Donnell, T Conway, G Friel, P Reilly, H Friel, B McDonald, P Friel, S Barrett, J Donnelly, Bro Cornelius Lean, P Boyle, F Irwin, M Friel, E Friel.[8]

Some of those involved in gaelic football also managed to form a hurling team, the Eugene O'Growney's.[9] Although the club found itself with little or no hurling opposition, they did play a match in Mussleburgh and encountered a number of University and College shinty sides (Edinburgh, Glasgow, Dundee College and a Perth based club) in compromise matches. A number of other clubs were also initiated during the 1950s. Roger Casements in Clydebank, St Francis' in Falkirk, St Patrick's Greenock and St Colmcille's in Edinburgh. Round Towers based in the Kildara Club, Earl Street in Scotstoun, and also Fintan Lalors Gaelic Football Club from Govan were also founded, the latter taking part in the 1954–55 championship.[10]

Players, championships and Pearse Park

In June 1950, Central Council in Dublin sponsored an exhibition gaelic football game at Moore Park, Govan, the home of St Anthony's junior soccer club: this between two senior county teams from Ulster, Derry and Antrim. The match ended Antrim 3:11, Derry 2:8. Teams and officials stayed at the Beresford Hotel, later to become part of Strathclyde University's Halls of Residence. The Ulster guests were welcomed by the Glasgow County Board at a ceili reception held at St Simon's Hall, Benalder Street, Partick in Glasgow. In addition, players and officials from both counties were taken as guests to visit Canon Taylor and the Lourdes Grotto at Carfin in Lanarkshire: this visit echoing the one half a century before when the Rapparees of Glasgow visited Sarsfields of Coatbridge, the visiting team being taken on tour of local Catholic schools and chapels.[11] On the same day as the visit to Carfin, a Glasgow team played a Derry-Antrim select at the gaelic park, Glenburn Stadium, Carfin.

Arising out of a visit to Scotland by Patrick McNamee, Ulster representative on the Central Council, Glasgow was included in the junior All-Ireland football Championship to play London at New Eltham Park, on August 23rd 1952. London narrowly won the match 1:10 to 1:8. At least eight of the Scottish based players had previously played county football in Ireland, including Hudai Beag Gallagher who had won Railway Cup medals in 1942 and 1943.[12] The Glasgow based side which represented Scotland was made up from the following players:

> Jerry Galvin (Roscommon), Tony Coll (Derry), K McSherry (Leitrim), Owen Kelly (Fermanagh), Tom Conway (Mayo), Sean Barrett (Monaghan), Pat O Meara (Tipperary), Con McKenna (Monaghan), Tony McGee (Fermanagh), John Doherty, Tommy Boyle, Hudai Beag Gallagher, Michael Friel, Paddy Boyle, Eddie McBrearty, Joe Rushe, Willie McGee, Paddy Diver and Tommy McGinley (all Donegal).

Further games took place in Ulster. In 1954 Glasgow played Antrim at Casement Park and later travelled to Clones to meet Monaghan. Despite the prestige attached to these games, success eluded the Glasgow based players.

One of the most significant events for gaels in Scotland and indeed, for the future revival of the Association, was the purchase of an area of land in Glasgow in 1953. The main driving force behind the purchase of the park was Charlie Quinn, although its buying was opposed by officials like Gerry Gallen who thought the area too isolated and believed there were already reasonable crowds attending matches at Carfin. Quinn had long anticipated a piece of land the Glasgow G.A.A. could call its own and in his capacity as a travelling foreman he searched for an appropriate piece of ground. An area at Eastfield in Cambuslang attracted him and it was soon purchased from people living in the U.S.A., relations of two elderly ladies from Glasgow who had previously owned the area.

Table 8.1
Glasgow Football Championship winners 1950–1958[13]

1949–50	Eire Og
1951–52	Pearses
1952–53	Clan na Gael
1953–54	Clan na Gael
1954–55	Pearses
1955–56	St Patricks
1956–57	Fintan Lalors
1957–58	Roger Casements

Although Quinn had viewed a pitch so heavy with water 'there were ducks swimming on it', he managed to arrange for a number of workers to partly revive the area, an effort mainly carried out in the evenings when the same workforce had previously finished their normal course of work. Soon after the purchase of the land a park was drained and turfed. Quinn's sister, Molly, paid for huts from a source in Motherwell and these were to become the dressing rooms for almost half a century.[14] A steering committee of Owen Kelly, John Keaveny, Rory Campbell, Charlie Quinn and Reverend P J McGovern of St Roch's Parish in Glasgow, helped raise money for the purchase of six and a half acres of ground. Campbell, McGovern and Padraig MacNamee, the first Ulsterman to head the G.A.A. at Croke Park, became the ground's patrons.

Due to Glasgow's prevarications, those representing the County had finally to pay more for the ground than the price initially quoted. Central Council of the G.A.A. in Dublin loaned the Glasgow G.A.A. £300. Owen Kelly added a loan of £50 to finally seal the deal whilst the committee raised the following donations:

Table 8.2
Pearse Park Financial Contributions 1953[15]

Fr P Burke	£2.00
Fr P J Brady	£2.00
Fr M Coakley	£1.00
Fr Gillespie	£1.00
Fr Hanrahan	£1.00
Fr M Lyne	£1.00
Fr Lowery	£5.00
Mr J McVey	£2.2s
Mr E McGowan	£1.1
Fr McHugo	£1.10
Mr J O'Byrne	£0.10
Fr Whyte	£1.10
Mr T Cassidy	£0.10
Mr F Carr	£0.10
Mr J Tonner	£0.10
Scottish Council, Anti-Partition League	£2.2
Fr O'Keefe	£2.2
Mr J McMenamin	£0.10
Fr Keegan	£1.00
Mr F Jordan	£1.1
J Colton	£3.15
J Kavanagh	£3.3
Fr D B White	£1.00
Fr Conway	£10.00
Chas Quinn	£10.00
Gaelic League	£20.00

The ground was formally opened with a match between Glasgow and opponents from Lancashire.

1960s–1970s

Despite the positive gains made by the G.A.A. in Glasgow, by the early 1960s the only gaelic sport manifest amidst the large Irish community in the west of Scotland took place at Eastfield Park, Cambuslang. At Cambuslang, individuals, mostly Irish born and with a strong Donegal influence, congregated at the pitch, picked sides and played matches. The main organisers were individuals like John Quaile, Gerry Gallagher, Eddie McBrearty, Charlie Quinn and Owen Kelly. However, the availability of players largely depended on how the building trade was functioning, many potential players involved in that industry. For one player during this era, the economic situation and the type of work in which many of the gaels were involved, meant that:

> there tended to be constant movement of gaelic footballers. Players could be available one week and not free for several weeks. If the family was based in Glasgow you could have one player one week and then the next he would appear with his brother. This made team selection difficult, but when it operated to your benefit with lots of players available the strongest side could be fielded.[16]

During 1962 one of the highlights for the G.A.A. in Glasgow took place when a seven-a-side tournament was participated in by around ten teams. In 1963, at a challenge match in Liverpool, the Glasgow Board played and defeated Lancashire Champions, John Mitchells'. Some of the players who participated in that victory were:

> Sean Sexton (Cavan), Paddy O'Donnell (Donegal), Paddy Boyle (Donegal), Gerry Galvin (Roscommon), Frank Corr (Donegal), Seamus and Pat Maguire (Donegal), Pat Kearney (Donegal), Eamonn Cullen (Donegal), John Brown (Donegal) and John Langan (Derry).

The following year a Scottish based side was well beaten by London in the British Provincial Championship. In 1964, Glasgow defeated John Mitchell's from Birmingham.[17] In 1965 a number of G.A.A stalwarts began training regularly at Eastfield Park. Eamonn Cullen (secretary), Clydebank priest Father Bartholomew Burns (Chairman), Sean Moore an Aer Lingus employee (assistant secretary) and Charlie Quinn (treasurer) made up the County Board for the season. St Eunan's, Padraic Pearses (which emerged from the Padraic Pearse Fianna Fail Cumann in Glasgow) and Clan na hEireann evolved to become the G.A.A. clubs of this particular period. The first championship of this era was won by the St Eunan's club which then went on to draw with John Mitchell's from Liverpool in the Provincial Championship. In 1966 County Antrim Champions St John's from Belfast visited Glasgow whilst St Eunans visited Manchester and defeated the local St Brendan's club. The same year also witnessed the start of a new club, Clydebank based St Brendans, who replaced the struggling Clan na hEireann team. This club was started by Father Burns, Eamonn Cullen and Owen Kelly. In 1966, St Eunan's again won the championship.

REGENERATION

Although only three clubs participated in the 1967 championship, gaels traditionally regard this season as a high point in the G.A.A. Glasgow years, with games being played on a regular basis at Eastfield Park. St Brendan's shocked holders St Eunan's to win the 1967 championship, and apart from four players from Tyrone and Monaghan, the winners panel consisted entirely of Donegal born players. The Scottish based champions were subsequently beaten by one point in a British Junior Championship semi-final against John F Kennedy's from Leeds. Such a strong Donegal representation was also reflected in the instigation of an annual Donegal players versus the rest of Ireland members played at Eastfield Park.

Visits to and from clubs in Ireland also characterised this era, and St Eunan's, Inch, St Joseph's Bundoran/Ballyshannon, Gweedore and Downings, all Donegal, Castleblaney Faughs Monaghan, South Kerry, St John's Belfast, Crossmaglen County Armagh, Clan na Gael Dublin, Bellaghy County Derry, John F Kennedy's Leeds and London Gaels all participated. In 1968 there remained three teams in Glasgow though Padraic Pearses quickly demised. They were soon replaced by another Glasgow club, Clan na Gael. That year St Brendan's retained the championship.

By 1969 St Eunan's club had demised, only to be replaced by another club, South O'Hanlons. One player in particular, Father Sean McGrath, a Fermanagh born priest and former county footballer based at the priest training college of Buchlyvie in Stirlingshire, providing the club with a much needed boost of talent and coaching. Nevertheless, it was Clan na Gael who won the championship in 1969. This season also witnessed Glasgow defeated in the Ulster Junior Championship by Down: the match held at Casement Park, Belfast. According to one participant of this period, the quality of the County team was never truly reflected in positive results due to the fact that a number of the accomplished players did not travel when county matches were played away from Glasgow.[18] A similar situation was also to handicap the County squad throughout the 1980s and 1990s as players were reluctant to contribute to County fortunes.

In relation to the quality of the game played in Scotland there were a number of players who had played both senior and minor football for their counties in Ireland; Neil Gallagher (Donegal), Anthony Gallagher (Donegal), Joseph Winston (Donegal), Tadg

71

McGinley (Donegal), Sean McGrath (Fermanagh), Chris Kane (Dublin) and Michael Power (Waterford) being the most prominent participants during this era. The most notable Scottish born players of the period were Joe Pugh and Eugene Herren (St Brendan's), Pat McInerrin and Michael Mulkerrin (St Eunan's) and Malky Mackay, John McGowan and Gerry Morrow of Clan na Gael. Mackay and McGowan were also soccer players with Queens Park whilst the son of the Mackay, also Malky, played with Celtic Football Club in the 1990s.

Table 8:3
Glasgow Football Championship winners 1965–1969

1965	St Eunan's
1966	St Eunan's
1967	St Brendan's
1968	St Brendan's
1969	Clan na Gael

To the detriment of the Association in Scotland, this period was also characterised at County Board level with a number of long acrimonious meetings. The Glasgow County concurred when the G.A.A. removed 'the ban' in 1971, despite the efforts of Owen Kelly to have the organisation in Glasgow vote against the move.[19] Over the course of the following decades, along with Rory Campbell, Kelly encouraged the resurfacing of elements in an approach to Irish culture which for many in the G.A.A. had become irrelevant and for some activists, were more appropriate for a time gone by.

In 1970 and 1971 the Glasgow Champions were accepted to play in the Ulster 'Club' championship. Around this time Glasgow played Clan na Gael of Armagh in the tournament. Although beaten 2:12 to 3:7 at Eastfield Park, Glasgow took great store from the fact that the winning club subsequently went on to become beaten finalists in the All-Ireland Club Championship.

By this time clubs in Glasgow were again experiencing a decline and subsequent reorganising. Much of this was to be the result of players and activists moving on to new employment in Britain or Ireland. The St Brendan's Club was one example of this reorganisation, soon becoming Mulroy Gaels, called after the bay of the same name in County Donegal. Other St Brendan's players formed Rosses Rovers (again called after a Donegal location)

72

whilst they also drew players from Clan na Gael. During this time Crossmaglen Rangers visited Glasgow to play in the Ulster Junior Championship. In the east of the country, Father Eugene O'Sullivan from Kilkenny tried to give birth to a hurling side though he had to settle for a shinty team. Some of the footballers from the Glasgow area went east and played in a number of challenge matches against O'Sullivan's charges.

Despite a small organisation, the three existing clubs in Glasgow engaged in much rivalry, this due in the main to the regional basis of the clubs. However, one former player of this era described the rivalry as sometimes distasteful.[20] Mulroy Gaels drew their players mainly from central and east Donegal. Significant figures for Mulroy were Seamus Sweeney, Eamonn Cullen, Donal McBride and John Connor. South O'Hanlons took most of their players from the six counties of Northern Ireland, while Rosses Rovers brought footballers from 'The Rosses' and west Donegal, although the club also contained players from other counties. Many of the Rosses team were Irish speakers and much intra-team communication was carried out in the native tongue.

One Rosses player became a significant figure in the future revival of the sport in the west of the country. Father Eamonn Sweeney, a native of Ballycroy, County Mayo, arrived at St Bridget's Baillieston in the east of Glasgow as a young curate in 1969. Drawn into the local G.A.A. by another Irish born priest, former seminarian colleague at St Peter's college in Wexford, Neil Carlin from Derry, Sweeney began to play in the small and poorly organised local competitions.

During this time clubs struggled to field regular sides and many games were played with teams lacking a full compliment. In 1970 the *Irish Weekly* newspaper included an article which attempted to revive the ailing Association in Scotland.

> As far as the clubs were concerned during 1970 the efforts of St Eunans and St Patricks as effective units were almost nil. Some individuals make token efforts, but no more. St Brendan's found themselves with no opposition....The G.A.A. in Glasgow hope to have a social centre at Eastfield Park before the end of 1971. The presence of such a centre would ensure regular football as well as providing the very necessary social amenities...[21]

Despite Sweeney's attempts and partial success in attracting local born players, a concerted effort to achieve this on the part of the Glasgow G.A.A. was absent. An exhibition game between a Donegal club side and a local select held at the Coatbridge home of Albion Rovers senior soccer team, which attracted a crowd numbering several hundred, failed to provide the impetus required. The ideas of Sweeney and his more forward looking fellow gaels, with respect to a more significant G.A.A. within the Catholic community in Scotland, had to remain a dream for the time being.

All for the Cause: Perceptions of Irishness in Scotland

Despite successes, during the forty years after the Second World War, clubs in Scotland also encountered many of the problems which plagued gaelic sports activity in previous years. Many of the Donegal immigrants in the Glasgow area were labourers and a significant number of them worked as tunnellers. This was a hard and dangerous employment often entailing weekend work, at a time when others were attempting to revive gaelic sports. This reflected in regular poor attendances for matches, occasional inferior standards of play and a general atmosphere of isolation. Progress was further impaired by a lack of publicity for Irish activities in Scotland and for gaelic sport in particular. For Liam Murphy, who played with Pearses in Glasgow, if the Irish were given media coverage it was frequently in a disparaging manner. However, more regularly the Irish were ignored, their distinctiveness not recognised and if Irish facets of life in Scotland were given attention, it was likely to be through a discourse and medium of sectarianism.

One example of the negative reporting of gaelic football in Scotland, in addition to the often stereotypical method of reporting things Irish, during Murphy's time took place in the wake of a seven-a-side gaelic football tournament at Roseberry Park, Shawfield, Glasgow in the 1950s.

> Gaelic football played by sturdy sons of the Ould Country wasn't quite what we expected...There are a multitude of rules, multiplied from football, I suspect, so that more rules can be ignored...they can kick it, punch it, EVEN HIDE it!...[22]

Forty years later such reporting on matters Irish prevailed. In 1991 the Sunday Scot, a short lived newspaper owned by Glasgow Rangers chairman, David Murray, ran a story headlined, 'Gael,

Gael, the Celts are here! The article was considered fair by enthusiasts in Glasgow, though several G.A.A. members were less positive about the articles introduction which alluded to stereotyped notions of, 'the stupid Irish'.

> The Sunday Scot looks at some of our zanier sports. The big centre controls the ball with his hand, swivels in the box and balloons the ball wildly over the bar — and the football crowd go *wild* with delight. Sounds a bit Irish…[23]

A Glasgow journalist, who actually proved a supporter of Irish cultural activities in the 1990s, also adopted stereotypical notions of a 'thick Paddy' language of degradation when reporting a Tyrone versus Dublin gaelic football exhibition match held in Glasgow in 1996. He wrote:

> …Tyrone rallied to end the game at a rather respectable scoreline of two goals and eight points for Tyrone to the Dubs' three goals and fifteen points. I know: it sounds daft and bear in mind that this is an Irish sport…[24]

Similarly, a Glasgow newspaper on reporting the upsurge in gaelic football activities in the West of Scotland, and relating the story to former international football goalkeeper Pat Jennings, of County Down Northern Ireland, declared:

> Where else but in Ireland would you hear a group of supporters shout 'Up Down'.[25]

A humorous story arising from a play on the juxtaposing of words opposite in meaning to each other. However, the phrase 'where else but in Ireland' explicitly refers to a British cultural stereotypical notion of the 'stupid' or 'thick' Irish. Writing about a gaelic football match in Glasgow between two of Ireland's best footballing counties, an Evening Times journalist spoke of two teams set to 'knock the daylights out of each other'.[26] Such frequent and widely acceptable techniques and formulas for reporting gaelic sports and matters Irish in general, has been unlikely to reflect the merits of gaelic sports or serve the promotion of Irishness amongst the offspring of the Irish in Scotland. This mode of media reporting on Irish manifestations has a complex but well established history. This history has had a significant effect upon Irish identity.

A more unreserved derogatory commentary on Ireland was made in 1985 by the then editor of the Daily Express, Sir John Junor (the latest in a series of such comments). Junor's remark provoked the following comment from an observer of Irish affairs:

> John Junors remark that he would rather go looking for worms in a dunghill than visit Ireland is but one example of a quite unrepentant anti-Irishness of so much of the Tory press.[27]

Reviewing the London Finsbury Park Fleadh (music festival) for a London newspaper in 1990, Stan Gebler Davies wrote that, 'the easiest way to learn Gaelic is to murder someone for the IRA'. The implication being that the subsequent period spent in the Maze/Long Kesh prison would enable a prisoner to learn the Irish language amongst those incarcerated for similar crimes, a well established past time for the prison's Republican inmates.[28]

A regular columnist in the most popular broadsheet in Scotland, *The Herald*, frequently invokes a 'thick Paddy' cultural stereo-typing, a refinement illustrated in the contemporary Irish joke. Writing of a bright young colleen looking for some information regarding an enquiry from a Scot working in Dublin, the colleen admitted there were no rules and regulations regarding the enquiry but would the enquirer still like a copy of the 'unwritten laws'. The same journalist also made mention of tickets for an Ireland — Scotland rugby international which cost ten punts and which he sardonically added, 'included admission'.[29] A spelling mistake on the part of an advertisement for Jury's Hotel in Glasgow was highlighted by the same journalist in 1996. This reporter's penchant for degrading Ireland and the Irish became more obvious when he told his readers to, 'bear in mind they are an Irish company'.[30]

Celtic Football Club's Irish identity has also been the object of the 'thick Paddy' sub-culture. A newspaper reported that after going through sound checks on the public address system came the following words from Celtic's stadium supervisor: 'if this announcement cannot be heard in your part of the stadium, please contact control'. A humorous story, and of course, just as well for Celtic's 'continuing links with Irish ways' added the newspaper.[31]

For some British media commentators, a meaningful bond between the Catholic faith and the people and country of Ireland including its diaspora, also provides a means to denigrate Ireland, Irish Catholics and the Catholic faith. In 1996, writing of Catholic clerical misdemeanours in the *Scottish Daily Mail* a journalist stated:

> I have never understood why Roman Catholic clergy, as distinct from their Protestant brethren, are expected to forsake the company of women. Especially since, as anyone who has eavesdropped in an Irish village pub well knows, so many of them don't.[32]

Stereotypes were in order when the *Observer Scotland* profiled new author and soon to be MP, Helen Liddell, who originates from the popularly known 'Catholic Irish' town of Coatbridge. This particular correspondent wrote: 'Sex in Coatbridge, after all, had been traditionally a very straightforward exercise in human reproduction, the result in days gone by of a healthy intake of Guinness at the Labour Club'.[33] The abuse of Ireland's national drink, a town with possibly the biggest percentage per head of people with Irish antecedents in Britain, the sexual morality of the Catholic Church, and the strong links between the Labour Party and Catholics in west-central Scotland dovetailed with an ethno-religious stereotype in this report in a considered quality Sunday newspaper.

In 1996, the *Scottish Daily Mail's* Bruce Anderson wrote of Irish European Union Commissioner Padraig Flynn. Anderson described Ireland thus:

> As soon as you arrive in Ireland, you leave the modern world. Every mile you travel west of Dublin is also a mile west of the 20th century…This is a pre-20th century economy, based on the pig and potato and presided over by the priest.[34]

In 1987 the same writer wrote of Ireland's Sean McBride, winner of the Nobel Peace Prize (1974), the Lenin Peace Prize (1977) as well as the American Medal for Justice among other prestigious tributes. Anderson wrote that McBride had two guiding principles throughout his career, 'the first was hatred of Great Britain, the second was a worship of violence'. In contrast, Oliver Tambo, former president of the ANC described McBride as 'a great beacon, guiding and assisting oppressed people to the path of national liberation and self-determination'.[35]

In Scotland, it has frequently been evident that to be seen as Irish, and often Catholic, has meant that relevant attributes are assessed in negative terms. This has resulted in a significant denigration of Irishness in Scotland but also, as a reaction to this state of affairs, it has also meant problems relating to Irish identity being manifest within the G.A.A. in Scotland.

In the 1950s many members of the G.A.A. in Glasgow were also fervent Irish Irelanders. All things Irish were viewed not only in a positive light, but a strong element of executing Irish cultural practice in as pure a form as was demanded by such activists had to be adhered to and in some instances, was absolute. An aspect of this design for such activists was the strict enforcing of 'the ban'. Soccer and other 'anglicised' games and pastimes were forbidden, in terms of both participation and spectating, and this meant that people such as Rory Campbell and Owen Kelly were staunchly against 'foreign dances and entertainments'. This has also had the effect that despite Celtic Football Club being long adhered to by Catholic Irish immigrants and their offspring, for some gaels, Celtic was also looked on as being of a detrimental influence on the purity of Irish identity. A consequence of such perceived 'idealism' meant that many potential players were excluded from the G.A.A. in the cause of creating a particular image of being 'truly Irish'.

The pre-occupations of some G.A.A. activists in west-central Scotland with their ideas of an exclusive Irish identity, meant that people like John Keaveny eventually lost interest in the local gaelic scene. Although the years of 'the ban' had relevance to the situation in Ireland and was supported by the G.A.A. in Glasgow, in Scotland, Keaveny and many other Irish were supporters of Celtic Football Club. The enforcement of the ban in Scotland meant that as Chairman of the Association he could not attend soccer matches. However, as his young children began to mature, like many others of Irish origins they wished their father to take them to view Celtic matches. Partly in response to changing circumstances, as a retort to a distinct lack of organisation and leadership on the County Board, the practice of County Board members ignoring the conventions of time in an industrialised society and, with a frequent lack of discipline on the field of play, by the mid 1950s Keaveny left the Association. During the same period Gerry Gallen was also frustrated at the length of County Board meetings which 'seemed to talk of nothing and which resulted in a number of fruitless arguments'.[36] Gallen too eventually faded from G.A.A. activities in Glasgow.

Keaveny observed that extreme actions on the part of some Irish

78

_Celtic

Irelanders meant that many Irish were excluded from activities which were in fact, keenly Irish. Keaveny cites one example of Irish exclusivism, when in the 1950s at an Irish ceili in Glasgow, a crowd from Greenock arrived to enjoy the function: all were of Irish origin. However, few had experience of ceili dancing and some requested the 'Pride of Erin Waltz'. An argument ensued because some organisers felt their Irishness was being compromised. This antagonism resulted in the Greenock participants refusing to return to further ceili's.[37] Such occurrences has parallels with the Irish experience of half a century before when, in 1914, a G.A.A. official complained of the vast majority of G.A.A. members whose, 'nationalist sentiment begins and ends with the mere practice of kicking or striking a hurling ball'.[38] Such individuals invariably believed they set the standards for being Irish and everyone else was required to match them.

In the 1990s several members of Irish community organisations continued to maintain such rigidness in their definitions of being Irish. In March 1994, an incident was caused by a self-imagined 'Irish Irelander' at a G.A.A. function held in Coatbridge. The reception included a presentation of the Sam Maguire trophy brought to Scotland by Micky Moran, coach of 1993 All-Ireland Football Champions, Derry. A member of the Gaelic League confronted a local G.A.A. activist regarding two guests not standing at the end of the evening for the playing of the Irish national anthem. Both individuals concerned had in fact Irish born parents, but they had little appreciation of the cultural practices of the G.A.A. Nonetheless, the League activist stated he would not return to a function held by this particular G.A.A. club. As far as this 'Irish Irelander' was concerned, the club had not pursued this cultural practice with enough vigour.[39]

One writer on gaelic sports in Ireland has intimated that such cultural exclusivism in adhering to a strict and formal interpretation of rules, and meanings of gaelic sport in particular, has been a mistake, because it closed doors and created an ideal of purity which became exclusivist and narrow minded.

> It's an old Irish failing to become precious about these things. You can only speak Irish if your born to it. Irish dancing isn't Irish dancing unless the participants are standing ramrod straight and stiff as corpses. Sean nos isn't sean nos unless its boring.[40]

Although Irish cultural activities were often required to operate within a variety of limitations and constraints imposed by the wider society, and the response to these circumstances were often correspondingly strict, other factors have also contributed to an often diminishing Irishness in Scotland. Former G.A.A. activist Liam Murphy describes his parents as having no real purpose for passing on their heritage to their children. He believes that one of the reasons for this lay in their lack of formal education resulting in an inability to pass on an articulate and positive sense of and affinity for, Ireland. They also lacked a corresponding motivation, viewing their children as Scottish in that this was the best way to social acceptance, achievement and progress.

John Keaveny's experience were similar to Murphy's parents in that his children were 'left to their own devices'. He recognised problems that Irish people had in Scotland and even encountered some of them himself. Although also recognising that Scotland was a foreign land and a certain accommodation in attitudes had to take place amongst the Irish corresponding to their changed situation, he maintained caution in things Irish by 'being very careful here'.[41] A further insight into this kind of approach to a new life in Scotland was implicit in a Donegal immigrants experience in Glasgow, when she spoke of losing her Irish language and learning English. She described this as learning to speak 'better'.[42] Murphy's father believed his son would find life difficult in Scotland if his background was known. He was surprised to find him earning an apprenticeship with a printing firm, a trade then popularly known to be almost exclusively Protestant. Experiences such as Murphy's and those of the Donegal migrant, who viewed loss of her native language as 'progress', are occurrences which invariably affected the self perceptions as well as self esteem of many Irish in Scotland, particularly during the periods of overt hostility during the 1920s and 1930s.

In some of the experiences of black people in the U.S.A. sentiments can be uncovered which relate a similarity in the lack of ability to understand and express identity, heritage or culture, amidst Irish people in Scotland. Marsha Hunt, a well known personality in the U.S.A., only discovered she was a black negro while watching a TV show as a child. She commented to her mother, that 'negroes are the funniest people'. Hunt's mother then informed her that she was a negro. Hunt's response was to deny this.

What I actually meant that I had heard so many disparaging things about negroes that I did not associate that or my family with colour. I associated it with some sort of state of being that I had nothing to do with.[43]

The experience of those like the Donegal migrant and of Murphy's reflects that some Irish in Scotland thought that the best or the only way to make social progress in Scotland, was in disguising much of their Irishness and privatising many aspects of their past as well as their experiences and identities. Indeed, for many Irish who encountered hostility which seemed to reduce their own and their families' life chances, Irishness was substantially discarded or became a factor of a past which represented poverty and oppression. Some immigrants felt the need to hide their place of origin in Ireland: this in case they were sent back home 'or there was a clampdown by the authorities on the number of people entering the country'.[44] A significant number of Catholics of Irish origins in today's west-central Scotland have little knowledge regarding the place of birth of their grandparents and great grandparents. In some extreme cases this also applies to Irish born parents.[45]

Early in the 20th century, P T McGinley of the Gaelic League castigated those Irish who came to the west of Scotland. He said many of them,

> abandoned their native language and customs, in the belief that the civilisation they found around them was superior to their own. In adopting the speech and habits of their neighbours, they forgot their origins and became anglicised....[46]

As a cultural activist McGinley had a point to make, especially during a time of struggle to maintain the very notion of being distinctly Irish, even in Ireland. The Irish perceived themselves as being oppressed and down trodden for centuries. Although many people throughout the 19th and 20th centuries would be of a similar mind to McGinley and participated in Irish ways and activities and often retained a strong sense of Irishness, it was the 1980s and 1990s before Irishness assumed a widespread confidence which disturbed the previous consequences and effects of the initial perceptions, which had critically affected and partly shaped Irish identity throughout the period of colonisation and after.

Despite understanding his existence as ghetto like, and his

Some children didn't know they were Irish

social contacts often being limited, Liam Murphy actually only became aware of being Irish when, after leaving school at fourteen, he was sent to carry out some work in the Fianna Fail club in Glasgow. There he met other young men of his own age group. They all had similar backgrounds which became a matter of conversation and subsequent learning. Questions began to be asked at home and Murphy developed a stronger sense of Irishness. Born in Glasgow and married to a Kilkenny woman, Liam Murphy's parents were in fact resolutely Irish, originating from Belmullet in County Mayo, an area retaining a positive traditional identity. They were also Republicans, his father being a former member of the Irish Republican Army during the War of Independence and his mother being a member of Cumman na Bann, the women's side of the movement. Both were to take the anti-treaty side during the Irish Civil War. However, Liam heard little of politics at home. Only in visiting Ireland, reading books and attaining an independence as he got older did his Irishness as well as his Irish political views begin to form.[47]

For others like Rory Campbell, as a second generation youth in the 1930s and 1940s in Glasgow, the only way to confidently display his Irishness was, as for many others, supporting Celtic Football Club. During this period he found:

> no other way to be Irish...there was nothing around with a semblance of Irishness involved...but gradually, the scales fell off my eyes.[48]

Later, Campbell was to find other avenues to being Irish in Scotland. Over the course of the next fifty years, he became an active member of the G.A.A., the Gaelic League (Conradh na Gaeilge, Glaschu), Comhaltas Ceoltoiri Eireann (Music and Musicians of Ireland) as well as Sinn Fein and Republican prisoners welfare groups.

Campbell's main contribution to Irish affairs in Scotland has been through his involvement with the Gaelic League. Rory Campbell views this aspect of Irish culture as being of primary importance and indeed recognises that learning the language of antecedent generations means one can learn the 'spiritual values of the past... it binds us to past generations'. Although rarely a gaelic player, Campbell held a number of offices within the Glasgow, and subsequently Scotland G.A.A., in the half century since the Second World War. In 1997, Campbell was a member of the G.A.A. in Scotland in the capacity of Irish language representative, and in the G.A.A.s centenary year, sole surviving member of the trustees of Pearse Park. By the time of the G.A.A.s centenary in 1997, Campbell remained one of the only operative links with previous generations of G.A.A. activists in Scotland.

Packy O Donnell was contemporary of Campbell's most active G.A.A. days. As a fourteen year old, O Donnell arrived in Scotland from Dungloe, County Donegal, to join his father labouring in Glasgow. O Donnell also married into the Irish community of the West of Scotland, uniting with Kathleen Gillespie, niece of Tom Gillespie who had been so important to Irish cultural activities in Glasgow during the period shortly before the Second World War. From the mid 1960s through the 1990s, Kathleen's 'O Donnell's School of Irish Dancing' organised classes in the Glasgow area and competed at a number of Irish dancing world championships.

Irish Dancing brought to Scotland [handwritten annotation]

O Donnell was one of the top players in Glasgow during a period noted for its high quality of experienced gaelic sportsmen. However, as for other stalwarts of the 1940s and 1950s, married life and children impacted on the time and commitment these young players could devote to gaelic football. Although being an ever present on the football scene for ten years until around 1958, like many other immigrants to the West of Scotland, O Donnell also found that through his children he became involved in another Irish pastime of supporting Celtic Football Club: his sons interests being similar to many other young second generation Irish. Although O Donnell recognised his family as retaining strong links with the family's origins, especially through holidays in Ireland and in his wife's Irish Dance School, and despite some involvement with the annual sports day held at Pearse Park in the 1970s, none of his family maintained a link with gaelic sport. During O Donnell's active days, few within the Glasgow G.A.A. had the foresight to expand the game to 2nd and 3rd generation Irish.

GAA didn't pass down family tree [handwritten annotation]

Standing out among the other main links with previous periods is Owen Kelly. Born in Ederney, County Fermanagh, aged eighteen Kelly emigrated to Glasgow in 1946. His father was also an earlier migrant, working in Coatbridge's Phoenix Foundry in the first decades of the 20th century. Kelly senior participated in hurling competitions involving Coatbridge clubs at this time. While working in Coatbridge he noted that a significant number of immigrants involved in gaelic sport originated from the province of Munster. Like many other immigrants, Owen Kelly married a woman of Irish antecedents: her parents originating from Tyrone and Donegal. For almost fifty years Kelly has been a gaelic enthusiast, involving himself first with Paisley Gaels in the late 1940s, being instrumental in the purchase of Pearse Park, and along with Jimmy McHugh of Tyrone, was a founder member of the Irish Minstrels, the first branch of Comhaltas Ceoltoiri Eireann outside of Ireland. Since the purchase of Pearse Park, but particularly since the 1970s, despite the dilapidated facilities, Kelly has also been important in maintaining Pearse Park as a gaelic football venue in the west of Scotland.[49]

Notes

1. Wilson, 1988. p. 149.
2. Dermot Gillespie subsequently emigrated to Canada from Scotland.
3. Interview, Rory Campbell.
4. The Fermanagh Herald, 23/1/1993.
5. This club demised in 1951.
6. Gallen was also manager of the Irish Club, formally the Top Hat Club, St Georges Road, situated in Glasgow's Charing Cross area. In the late 1950s this was a popular venue for early Irish folk groups as well as many of the show bands of the era.
7. Irish activist Rory Campbell remembers that although not overtly political, a number of the teams during this period were known as either republican or Fianna Fail clubs. He believes this was probably a reflection of the dominant views of their prominent members at the time. For some activists such as John Keaveny, he did his utmost to keep politics out of G.A.A. affairs during this period.
8. Glasgow G.A.A. Centenary Brochure, 1984.
9. O Growney being one of the founders of the Gaelic League.
10. The Kildara Club was formally a hall of the A.O.H. and latterly owned by the O Neill family which ran a school of Irish dancing in the city. The family moved eventually to the U.S.A.
11. Glasgow G.A.A. Centenary Brochure, 1984. Interviews John Keaveny and Gerry Gallen.
12. Glasgow G.A.A. Centenary Brochure, 1984.
13. Ibid.
14. Interview Molly Quinn. Quinn was also to make football shorts from flour bags purchased at Glasgow's Barrowland Market for Clan na Gael Football Club.

15. Ibid.
16. Ibid.
17. Ibid.
18. Ibid.
19. In Ireland twenty-eight of the thirty county boards voted in favour of 'the bans' removal.
20. Interview Father Eamonn Sweeney.
21. Irish Weekly.
22. Sunday Mail, August 1954.
23. Sunday Scot, 23/6/1991.
24. Jack McLean in The Herald 'Sport', 25/3/1996.
25. Herald, September 1996.
26. Reported in the Irish Post, 27/2/1993
27. Reported by Donal MacAmhlaigh, Ireland's Own 5/7/85
28. Irish Post 25/8/90
29. Tom Shields, The Herald 17/1/96 p. 15
30. The Herald 9/1/96, p. 21
31. The Herald 9/2/96, p. 21
32. Keith Waterhouse, Scottish Daily Mail 23/9/96 p. 12
33. Observer 'Scotland', 10/6/90, p. 8
34. Scottish Daily Mail 1/11/96 p. 8
35. Irish Post 9/11/95 p. 8
36. Interviews John Keaveny and Gerry Gallen.
37. Interview John Keaveny.
38. Rouse, 1996.
39. Interview member of Sands MacSwiney's G.F.C.
40. Humphries, 1996, p. 39.
41. Interviews, John Keaveny and Gerry Gallen.
42. Jimmie MacGregor, 'Across the Water' BBC Radio Scotland, four part series, 1st–22nd November, 1995.
43. Marsha Hunt, 'God Bless America', ITV 24/3/1997.
44. Cassidy, 1996, pp. 34–38.
45. Ongoing research into Irish identity in Scotland has reflected huge numbers of interviewees do not recollect where in Ireland their relations originated. In one example this extended to an elderly lady's father who she knew as having immigrated from Ireland but was unaware from where in Ireland he originated.
46. Feeney 1995.
47. Interview Liam Murphy.
48. Interview Rory Campbell.
49. Interview Owen Kelly.

7. Thomas Davis, Motherwell. c. 1948.

8. Paisley Gaels, c. 1950.

9. *Pearses, Glasgow, 1952.*

10. *Glasgow Team* v. *London. Junior All-Ireland Football Championship, 1952.*

11. Glasgow County Team, 1964.

12. Clan na Gael, Hamilton, 1985.

13. Pearse Harps, Glasgow, 1986.

14. Mulroy Gaels, Glasgow, 1989.

15. Beltane Shamrocks, Wishaw, 1989.

16. Sands MacSwineys, Coatbridge, 1989.

17. Cuchuluins's Glasgow, 1992.

18. Glencovitt Rovers, Clydebank, 1992.

19. Dundee Dalriada, 1993.

20. Dunedin Connolly's, Edinburgh, 1994.

21. Coatbridge Gaels, 1995.

22. St Patrick's, Dumbarton, 1996.

23. Scotland under-16 Team v. Warwickshire, 1996.

24. Paisley Gaels, 1996.

25. Scotland County Squad 'Irish International Football Tournament', Dublin, 1996.

26. Tir Conail Harps, Glasgow, 1997.

27. Shotts Gaels, 1997.

28. Shotts Gaels, Camogie, 1997.

CHAPTER 9

IRISH CULTURAL REVIVAL IN SCOTLAND

> Games and athletic contests offer a dramatic commentary on reality
> rather than an escape from it. [They are] a heightened re-enactment
> of communal traditions, not a repudiation of them.[1]

1984: Year of Resurgence

There was little G.A.A. activity in Glasgow during most of the 1970s
and early 1980s. During these barren years for gaelic sports in
Scotland, priests such as Eamonn Sweeney, Dominic Towey from
Kilmovee in County Mayo and James Friel of Derry, tried to keep
matters gaelic alive in Glasgow. In particular, Eamonn Sweeney
became a crucial figure in the latest regeneration of the Association
in Scotland. Other activists, some based in the Glasgow Irish
Centre in Glasgow's Govanhill area, also helped begin a revival.

An occasional exhibition match against an English based club
was all gaelic football witnessed in Glasgow during this time. For
gaelic enthusiasts like Glasgow based Mayoman, Michael Moran,
his desire to play organised football was only satisfied in his
travelling regularly to Huddersfield in Yorkshire to play with
Brothers Pearse. Since 1975 the annual Pearse Park family sports
day and reunion involving a gaelic exhibition match, a few
organised games for children and the celebration of mass, seemed
all Irish gaels in Glasgow could initiate. At this event a few hundred
people attended, with a strong Donegal representation being
present. This event characterised the G.A.A. in Scotland, in reality,
an organisation of little relevance to the majority of the immigrant
diaspora in the west of Scotland.

Few second and third generation Irish who esteemed their Irish
identity were aware of the G.A.A. in Glasgow or even that there
existed such a way to express Irishness, distinct from, or
complimentary to, supporting Celtic Football Club. Although a
small group of gaels had maintained the game throughout the
1960s and 1970s, the G.A.A. in Glasgow had little by way of
organisation or development plan. The organisation was limited
by numbers, little publicity, and an unrepresentative group in

that most were activists of latter Donegal origins. Although Donegal sent thousands of immigrants to the Glasgow area, particularly in the post war years, many more immigrants from other counties existed in Scotland. The question remains as to whether others with Irish identity were partly excluded from participating in gaelic games because of the unintentional parochialism which emerged from the overly Donegal based scene: officials and players being content to play football virtually among themselves. The greatest handicap for the G.A.A. in Scotland was its apparent inability to reach out to second and third generation immigrants who knew little of Eastfield Park or gaelic games in Scotland or Ireland.

During the mid to late 1970s a further effort was made to give life to Irish cultural affairs in Glasgow. Following the example of many Irish communities in England, and wishing to reinvigorate much of the social spirit of the past, a number of Irish cultural activists in Glasgow, including members of the G.A.A., attempted to create conditions required for an Irish social club in the city. Although there existed numerous Irish pubic houses as well as clubs frequented mainly by Celtic football supporters or Catholics of Irish antecedents, no formalised structure existed in the city or its environs. As part of a plan to change this situation and re-organise and facilitate expressions of Irish identity in the Glasgow area, Irish cultural activists such as Margaret O Dell helped raise money to purchase a new centre at Coplaw Street in the Govanhill area of Glasgow.[2] Although for a time providing a social and cultural focus for Irish functions, by 1982, as a result of poor management and serious financial difficulties, the resultant club was eventually forced to close[3]. Similarly, in 1984, a branch of the highly successful Irish in Britain Representation Group (I.B.R.G) was also formed in Glasgow, but it too demised after only a few years.

Eastfield Park was renamed Pearse Park in 1979:[3] this to celebrate the centenary of the birth of one of Ireland's foremost patriots and one of the leaders of the 1916 Easter Uprising. Padraic Pearse had a deep love for all things gaelic and of course had been a visitor to the city's Gaelic League in 1899 and 1902.[4] Linking with the parks renaming, to mark the centenary a joint G.A.A. and Pearse Centenary Committee organised the raising of funds to erect a Celtic Cross at the ground. A match was also played between a Glasgow team and Huddersfield, the winning Glasgow team receiving the Pearse Cup as its prize.

In 1984, Glasgow G.A.A was invited to play in an 'Exiles Tournament' in Ballina, County Mayo. Held under the auspices of the Croke Park authorities, this was a tournament intended to help celebrate the founding of the Association one hundred years before. Set in August, and also involving representative sides from New York, the rest of the U.S.A., Australia, London and the Rest of England as well as other teams from Ireland, the Glasgow team failed to field a Scottish based team: their Donegal based playing contingent not arriving for the opening match. Frank Conway, Eamonn Sweeney, Mick Moran (all Mayo) and Harry Cook, from Sweeney's parish in Baillieston outside Glasgow (whose parents derived from Donegal and Kerry), made up the Scottish contribution, additionally supplanted with players rounded up in the short time immediately before the game. For Father Sweeney, this negative experience further emphasised that a Scottish base had to be built if gaelic football was to flourish amongst the Irish in Scotland.

Around the same time, the small G.A.A. in Glasgow decided to celebrate the centenary of the Association by holding a special function. This celebration was held at the Knights of St Columba Club in Moodiesburn, outside of Glasgow. Moreover, for some members of this group such events presented an opportunity and inspiration to attract more individuals to the sport. Along with Eamonn Sweeney, successful Glasgow based Donegal building and demolition contractor Seamus Sweeney and fellow county man Eamonn Cullen, these G.A.A. enthusiasts decided to give birth to teams in their respective areas of Glasgow and Dumbarton.

In 1984 the *Evening Times* in Glasgow carried an article on a young girl from Ireland who had come to Glasgow for bone marrow treatment. Playing a role in the story, Eamonn Sweeney was interviewed by the free-lance journalist and he used the opportunity to draw the attention of the reporter to gaelic football activities in the area. What resulted was a degree of publicity and essentially an advert for people to learn to play gaelic football. A handful of young people responded and training and coaching under the auspices of Father Eamonn Sweeney and Michael Moran began. Those who arrived at Pearse Park trained over the course of the year until they comprised a team. Taking the name Pearse

Harps, because of their base at the G.A.A. ground in Cambuslang Glasgow, the club began to play challenge matches against the other developing teams, Mulroy Gaels, St Patricks of Dumbarton and Sweeney's new parish club, Clann na Gael based at St Ninian's, Hamilton. By the following year the first competitions began and gaelic football was re-born in the west of Scotland. In early 1985 four clubs, Pearse Harps and Mulroy Gaels from Glasgow, St Patrick's Dumbarton and Clann na Gael from Hamilton were competing in the first competitive league and championship set up for a generation.

By 1997, gaelic clubs had functioned in Glasgow, Coatbridge, Edinburgh, Saltcoats, Wishaw, Shotts, Paisley, Clydebank and Dundee. A number of under age clubs also began in these areas. Initiatives such as these were recognised by the Croke Park authorities who choose Scotland as the county to experiment with a two year pilot development scheme in 1995. Financed by the Dublin authorities, the scheme, was launched jointly by the Scotland County and Croke Park (including G.A.A. president Jack Boothman), at a reception held in Glasgow's Civic Chambers. For gaelic sports in Scotland, the intention of the Scotland Board related to the pursuit of avenues for sports funding to upgrade the dilapidated pitch and changing facilities at Pearse Park: the first step which the County required regarding recognition on the part of the Scottish Sports Council. The main benefits to Scotland were linked to the expansion and betterment of its games, including a hope of the appointment of a full time coach financed by the Dublin authorities, whilst Croke Park used the scheme to gain experience in best procedures for overseas development.

At the 1992 Glasgow County convention, a motion was proposed by Dundee Dalriada which again reflected the growth in gaelic sports in Scotland as well as the greater geographical spread since the late 1980s. Although the motion to name the County Board the Scottish County Board was defeated, an amendment by Sands MacSwiney's delegates that the principal of adopting a more encompassing name which resonated with the games development and greater geographical spread should be adopted: thus the name of the county was changed from the Glasgow Board to the County Board of Scotland[5]

Along with the County chairmanship of John McCreadie of Ayrshire Gaels in the early 1990s, and the subsequent chair work

100

and enterprise of secretary being carried out by Jimmy Kelly, John Nally and Charlie McCluskey, the County Board of Scotland acquired a degree of proficiency during this period. The participation of Tommy Main in the G.A.A. was also significant. Since his involvement in G.A.A. affairs, Main initiated and contributed to a higher public profile for the Association and also organised or assisted in the organisation of a wide range of Irish cultural activities in the west of Scotland, but particularly in Glasgow. Although some ventures have been short lived this was mainly a reflection of too few individuals dealing with an expanding Irish cultural scene. Amongst Main's achievements has been his involvement with a number of successful Strathclyde Irish Festivals since 1989, and which included a range of Irish cultural activities: ceilis, G.A.A. events, academic lectures, theatre, Irish dancing, concerts and bookfares. In 1988 he was instrumental in constituting an Irish Marian Day at Carfin Grotto in Lanarkshire and in 1991 also organised a Scor competition involving most G.A.A. clubs. In 1994 Main became one of the founders of the largest G.A.A. club in Scotland, Tir Conail Gaels.

In 1989 a Glasgow County representative squad travelled to New York to play in an international seven-a-side tournament. Headed by Father Eamonn Sweeney, the Glasgow team lost three matches during the course of a poorly organised competition. However, a high point for the County Board of Scotland, formed from the old Glasgow County Board, was the participation of a representative side in 1994 and 1996 in a prestigious international gaelic football competition held in Dublin under the auspices of the G.A.A. authorities at Croke Park. This competition has been recognised by the Dublin authorities as of crucial importance to those of the diaspora who promote this aspect of Irish culture abroad. In 1994, an under strength Scotland were defeated by London 0:24 to 1:4 and the North American Board 4:15 to 0:8. Scotland defeated Canada 0:11 to 1:7 in the play-off for last place. Included amongst the various dignitaries who attended some of the related functions for the 1996 tournament were, G.A.A. Uachtaran, Chairman of Bord Failte, the Lord Mayor of Dublin and the Minister for Tourism and Trade. Taking part in the tournament for the Dr Dermot Clifford Cup, which was held at the grounds of Dublin based St Enda's of Ballyboden, were gaelic football sides from Australasia, Canada, London, New York, North America (eventual winners) and the Rest of Britain, as well as from Scotland. Scotland lost both matches against North America (3:12 to 0:5) and the London County (0:5 to 0:15), but participation in both the inaugural tournament in 1994 and the subsequent competition in 1996, reflected the progress of gaelic football in Scotland since 1984.[6]

The promotion of such a tournament also showed a recognition of the place which the diaspora has in the progress of gaelic games. An increasing recognition of the Irish beyond the shores of Ireland by Irish President Mary Robinson also characterised her term of office during the 1990s. Jack Boothman, President of the G.A.A. during 1996, also recognised what the Irish have given to other lands as well as what Ireland has contributed to a sense of self and community for those who have had to leave the country.

> ...when one considers the tragedy of emigration and the great haemorrhage of our people to foreign lands. They brought with them to those lands their music, their culture and above all the legacy that is the G.A.A. and Gaelic Games. In turn, the G.A.A. provided them with a focus, a link with their homeland and a medium that stimulated togetherness and a sense of identity.[7]

During the 1990s some third tier educational establishments became involved in Scottish competition, hoping to compete at British universities level and ultimately, since 1997, to compete in the Irish Universities competition, the Trench Cup. Teams from Stirling, Glasgow, Ayrshire, Strathclyde, Dundee, Abertay and Aberdeen universities competed at this level during the 1990s. By 1997 twenty-eight universities across Britain were involved in these competitions. Many of the students taking part in university competitions are also members of local G.A.A. clubs. In Scotland, the most obvious example of this was the close relationship between Dundee and Abertay Universities and Dundee Dalriada. In 1993, Dundee won the British Universities Gaelic Football competition.

Although there has been a series of falls, steady and sometimes dramatic progress has been made since 1984. Hundreds of young Irish born, hundreds more of second, third and fourth generation Irish offspring, as well as others from outside the community, have participated in gaelic games in the west of Scotland as well as at a few locations in the east of the country. A number of Glasgow and Lanarkshire schools have adopted the game. A women's team existed as well as a camogie and hurling set up in Glasgow.

In 1992 a Pearse Park Redevelopment Committee was set up as a sub-committee of the County Board with the remit of raising funds for this purpose. Individuals involved in with the G.A.A. in Scotland such as Tim Porter (Scotland County Board), Billy Nugent (Sands MacSwiney's), Jimmy Kelly (Glencovitt Rovers), Peter Mossey (Dundee Dalriada), Mick Hollinger (Paisley Gaels), as well as Maurice Roachford (Aer Lingus), Niall Loakman (A.I.B. Bank), Paul Cunningham (Jury's Pond Hotel), John Nally, Charlie McCluskey, John Toal and John Gallagher (unaffiliated) contributed much unpaid time to Pearse Park's redevelopment.

The Kilkenny visit of eighty years ago was surpassed by the visits of Donegal, Derry, Mayo and Dublin during the 1990s: three of the four having been recent winners of All-Ireland football titles. In 1993, in front of approximately 2,000 spectators at St Aloysius Rugby Ground in the Millerston area of Glasgow, Donegal beat Mayo. In 1994 the north-west county defeated Derry and in 1995 it was Dublin's turn to be vanquished by the Ulster side. In 1996, the challenge took place between Tyrone and Dublin, the latter winning the Willie Dowds Trophy in front of around 1,000 people. An inter-county Celtic challenge cup has also been played for by a number of minor teams prior to each of these games. At a variety of Glasgow hotels, successful banquets were also held on the evening of the respective matches.

Ostensibly these visits have been concerned with raising money to finance the cost of the restoration of Pearse Park in Glasgow, a ground not only handicapped by a poor surface and lack of volunteers to provide maintenance, but which was also dilapidated by virtue of no suitable changing facilities. Within G.A.A. circles, it was generally felt that something should be done for the ground or the apparent potential for the games development would be lost.

> If developments at Pearse Park do not proceed soon, Irish identity may not be enough to hold on to their [i.e., youngsters involved in G.A.A. activities] loyalty. At present we just cannot compete with soccer, rugby or any other leisure pursuits in terms of playing and after-match facilities.[8]

As a contribution to the celebration of its centenary year, in April 1997, the County Board of Scotland welcomed the visit to Glasgow of County Sligo. Subsequently a gaelic football match between the Scotland County and Sligo took place at St Aloysius Rugby Ground. The match finished with a convincing victory by the visitors of 7:21 to 1:4: Sligo winning the Willie Dowds Cup which until then had been played for between counties from Ireland visiting Glasgow. For the fourth year in succession, Scotland minors defeated their opponents in the Celtic Cup: this time they beat Lancashire 5:11 to 0:4. The Sligo squad were hosted by Sands MacSwiney's over the course of their weekend in Scotland and completed their visit with attendance at the Scottish premier league soccer game played between Celtic and Aberdeen.

By the time the G.A.A. in Scotland celebrated the founding of its first club in Glasgow in 1897, there had emerged a new confidence and articulation in relation to Irish identity amongst the Irish diaspora. Therefore, the re-emergence of the G.A.A. in Scotland also links with a re-surfacing and articulation of Irish identity in many parts of Britain.[9] This development adds substance to the argument of Isajiw:

> Much evidence indicates in North America ethnic identities persist beyond cultural assimilation and that the persistence of ethnic identity is not necessarily related to the perpetuation of traditional ethnic culture. Rather, it may depend more on the emergence of ethnic 're-discoverers', i.e., persons from any consecutive ethnic generation who have been socialised into the culture of the general society but who develop a symbolic relation to the culture of their ancestors. Even relatively few items from the cultural past, such as folk art, music, can become symbols of ethnic identity.[10]

It has been recognised amongst some observers that a change has taken place amongst many second and third generation Irish in Britain in that many have began to reassert their Irishness and, to display it in a number of styles and forms which, as well as being traditional, have also been unconventional. These displays have also been less constrained by the established social and political pressures which being Irish in Britain has traditionally attracted.

Questions relating to Irish identity are important sub-themes of analysis into the history, development and role of the G.A.A. in

Scotland. Likewise, the history of the G.A.A. among the Irish diaspora, also gives credence to the arguments of a number of authors who believe that ideas of globalisation should be considered within a context of historical, cultural and spatial specificity.[11] The Association and its members retain a unique identity amidst a growing emphasis on 'global sports'. Gaelic sports remain a forum through which cultural, national and for some members, political identities, are projected, maintained and celebrated. Since the re-emergence of the G.A.A. in Scotland in 1984, many clubs have been founded and thousands of young people have experienced this aspect of Irish culture in Scotland.

Notes

1. C Lasch in The corruption of sports. New York Review of Books 24 (7) pp. 24–30, from Coakley, 1994, p. 25.
2. O Dell was for thirty years the longest serving president of the Gaelic League in Glasgow, was the prime mover in the revival of the annual St Brigid's Cross making in the city, assisted with the building of the Pearse memorial cross at Pearse Park, was much involved in Catholic Church activities and was formally a member of the Anti-Partition League in the West of Scotland. She was also associated with the visit to Glasgow of Eamon de Valera in the 1940s.
3. The Pearse Park Commemoration Committee consisted of Rev James Shiels, Sean Feeney, Rory Campbell, Rev Bernard Canning, Joseph Coyle, Rose Coyle, Margaret O Dell, Owen Kelly, Peter McAleer, Patrick O Donnell, Padraig Roarty and Lena Tierney.
4. B Canning, 1979.
5. Irish Post, 12/12/92, p. 34.
6. County Board of Scotland representatives at the international tournament in 1996 were; J Morkin, V Gleenan, S Quinn, E Brennan, M Brennan (Paisley Gaels), D Kellett, G Quinn, B Grimes, J Bradley, S McGinley, P Markey, R Gallacher (Sands MacSwiney's), R McHugh, B Grant, N Dillon, S Gavaghan, N Walsh, J McKeown, P Davies, M Joyce (Dunedin Connolly's), H Currie, D Nicol, J Hamill (St Patrick's) and D O Brien (Dundee Dalriada). M Hollinger (Paisley Gaels, Manager), S McGleenan (Sands McSwiney's Assistant Manager), K Friel (Paisley Gaels, Assistant Secretary) and I McGuigan (Paisley Gaels).

7. Jack Boothman, G.A.A. President, from programme for 'Irish Holidays International Football Tournament', 9th–13th Sep 1996.
8. T Main, Youth Development Officer, County Board of Scotland, from match programme for Donegal versus Mayo, 7/2/93.
9. See The Guardian, 16/7/96, p. 3 for reference to increase in Irish cultural activities in Scotland.
10. Isajiw 1974, pp. 111–124.
11. See Rowe and Wood, 1996, p. 524.

CHAPTER 10

GAELIC SPORT TODAY

Our games were in a most grievous condition until the brave and patriotic men who started the Gaelic Athletic Association took their revival in hand...Besides reviving our national sports, the G.A.A. has also revived national memories, the names of its clubs perpetuating the memory of many great and good Irishmen.[1]

Cultural, Nationalist and Patriotic Identities: Ireland

In the broadest understanding of the terms, the G.A.A. is a political and nationalist association, with inevitable Catholic cultural influences. However, the organisation has steered clear of overt political agitation allowing many shades of Irish Ireland, nationalist as well as non-patriotic opinion to come together. In its British-Irish context, Irish history has meant that the evolution of the G.A.A. has been strongly influenced by nationalist links. This means that the G.A.A. particularly appeals to patriotic minded people who view Irish nationalism as an important part of not only the Association but of their own identities. Nonetheless, the G.A.A. also considers itself to be non-party political, non sectarian and willing and able to embrace people from any background.

The political, cultural and religious aspects of the Association have largely been conditioned by the colonisation of the island of Ireland and its subsequent partition in 1922. Ultimately, this is the context which gave birth to the G.A.A. So long as there is a perceived artificial division of the north from the south and consequent British hegemony in relation to this division, as a national organisation which commands allegiance throughout the island on the basis of virtually ignoring many partitionist aspects of life in Ireland, in a broad and inclusivist fashion, invariably the G.A.A. is not only national but, nationalist.

The patriotic or nationalist identity of the G.A.A. has for many observers come to characterise it.

That the G.A.A. is national, and that the G.A.A. is involved — has always been involved — in the mainstream of Irish nationalism, is not in dispute...from the outset the social, cultural and national aspirations of so many of our people were embodied within the G.A.A. ethos. It was a national fusion, and, indeed it was as inevitable as it was desirable...This modern Association remains the product of a people's determination to pursue the Gaelic, the national tradition of these times. To promote the games, and, through the games, to work towards the national ideal was the Association founded. That role has been constant through the years. Today the Gaelic Athletic Association finds itself not the captive but rather the proud custodian of that tradition, that ideal. and is compelled by history to the continuing pursuit of the G.A.A. and the national ideal...In a word, in 1984 as in 1884, Nationalism and the Gaelic Athletic Association are indivisible.[2]

To the youth of Ireland, a knowledge of the circumstances in which the G.A.A. was founded, of the part it played in the years before the Rising of 1916, of the share its members had in the fight for freedom, is merely knowledge of their own inheritance and shall not be held from them. Such knowledge would mark out the native games as more than mere games and would show that the Association which promotes them has had, and still has, a strong influence for National good.[3]

The complex history of the G.A.A. mirrors that of Irish nationalism: it too has long been multi-dimensional and has often been conditioned by the peculiarities of context and the vicissitudes of British colonialism and domination in Ireland. For Humphries:

ties between Irish nationalism and the playing of gaelic games have never been severed. Nor will they be. As the sharp political edge of Irish nationalism recedes and is replaced by a softer but equally intense interest in the culture and language , the games of hurling and football are increasingly cherished as part of the national character. They come as part-and-parcel of a less threatening nationalism. As every yard of fibre optic cable and every bounced satellite beam shrinks the world, a small place without a vigorous language of its own can be pervious to every form of global blandness. Hurling and football are elements in which we preserve the root of ourselves.[4]

In Northern Ireland the G.A.A. is bound to the community in the same way it is to many people in the rest of the country. However, the differing circumstances give rise to differing consequences and the character of Northern Irish nationalism and patriotism means that the political edge of the G.A.A. is retained because it is viewed as relevant. Focusing on St Gall's Gaelic Club in Belfast, Humphries captures some of the reality of that Club's particular situation.

> St Gall's for instance, isn't composed of a group of people who have chosen Gaelic games from an extensive menu of leisure pursuits available to them. St Gall's, the club, the colours, the teams, represent a community, an area. Generations pass the club on to each other. What affects the community, affects the club.[5]

Likewise, during the course of the present troubles in Northern Ireland, a particularly stressful period for the Association, many clubs in the North have assisted in materially caring for members who have been drawn into the armed constituent of the conflict and have found themselves in prison. Much of this assistance arrives by way of looking after a member's family and will often be spurred on by local loyalty rather than for any wish to bring the Association undue hostility by appearing to be seen to favour 'armed struggle'. Although, undoubtedly some members will support this struggle, or at least will view it in a radically different way from much of British and even southern Irish opinion, the G.A.A. does not support this campaign. Indeed, like much opinion in Ireland it can be taken to be against its use. Reflecting the Association's attitude towards armed struggle, for one Republican inmate of Long Kesh/The Maze prison:

> Contrary to what people think, Republicans don't have a great opinion of the G.A.A. and what it has done nationally over the troubles. Clubs and families have been tight, but nationally the G.A.A. has been as apathetic as anyone else.[6]

Nonetheless, the nature of the Association means the overlap between culture and Irish history, past and present perceptions and reality, means the politics of change and cultural politics is inseparable.

In Northern Ireland, among many in the unionist population things Irish have long been held as alien, have been treated with great scorn and are further viewed as inhibiting and threatening due to their perceptible Catholic connotations. Although many British observers in the late 19th and early 20th centuries, and indeed many unionists/loyalists in present day Northern Ireland, have often viewed G.A.A. members as potential revolutionaries or terrorists awaiting the call of battle, Flanagan argues that:

this narrow-minded vision of the organisation, resulted in victimisation of the Association, its players and spectators by non-association members which has continued through the decades into Northern Ireland in the 1990s'.[7]

In County Down, teams' in Loughlinisland and Bryansford have had their club houses burned down whilst clubs' such as Bellaghy in County Derry had similar experiences during the past quarter of century or more of the Northern Ireland troubles. The situation in Crossmaglen County Armagh, where the British Army occupied the local Rangers club's ground for use as a helicopter landing pad, and in the late 1990s continued to have a major presence at the ground, is the most well known example of how the G.A.A. has been a significant focus in the conflict between Irish and British identities in the North of Ireland.[8] After winning the All-Ireland minor competition of 1987 the Down team passed through Clough on the way to Downpatrick: their bus was stoned by Loyalists. When the senior team passed through with the Sam Maguire four years later, as a matter of precaution all lights were dimmed in the team bus and in the town.

In 1991, despite large attendances and as the only major field sports during the Summer months, a Unionist councillor complained to the press there was 'too much Gaelic football being shown by the British Broadcasting Corporation'. Clubrooms at Ballycran in County Down were burned to the ground whilst North Down Borough Council voted not to send a letter of congratulations to Ulster Champions Down who had won the All-Ireland for the first time since 1968.[9] During May of 1997 the chairman of a County Antrim gaelic club was tortured and killed by loyalist paramilitaries, while the manager of a gaelic football club in north Belfast was killed in December of the same year.[10]

Historically, sporting conflict, or sport's links with wider elements of hostilities in Ireland, have not been confined to a cleavage between Irish and British identities as typified in gaelic sporting traditions. Many other sports have also been characterised or influenced by religious and political considerations. For example, Sugden and Bairner show this in relation to soccer and rugby, the latter having a 'pre-political cultural impact similar to the G.A.A., but operating in the opposite direction'. Likewise, the complex political situation in Northern Ireland means that the political dimensions of sport 'varies from sport to sport, from level to level and from one region to another'.

> Sport in itself is neutral, but because it can never be divorced from the politics of its players, administrators and supporters, it necessarily responds to the political currents of the habitat within which it thrives.[11]

Talking specifically about the G.A.A. in Northern Ireland, the same authors state:

> It would be a mistake to over-emphasise its formal political role, but, in a context where tradition and imagery are paramount, its potency both as a rallying point for Irish Catholics and a symbol of alien culture to northern Protestants is of great indirect political importance.[12]

In celebrating Irishness, gaelic sport has an inherent capacity to attract hostility from those who are repulsed by such expressions or who feel threatened by them.

Over the course of its history, for many people, the G.A.A. has been an important component of their nationalist identities. Historically, with the entire country embroiled in turmoil and conflict, the Association could hardly remain aloof from this. Indeed, it can be argued that conflict made the G.A.A. into a significant body in Irish life. After all, it was a perception of the clash between oppressed and oppressor, between native and usurper, which led to its foundation. In that experience, the Association's nationalist involvement, and many of its members participation in 'rebellious' activities which resulted from and produced a mixture of ideology and reaction to circumstances, has meant that the G.A.A. has been viewed as a focus for cultural and political resistance: that is, cultural and political nationalism.

Nevertheless, even if many aspects of culture in Ireland have been significantly politicised, it would be a narrow assessment to conclude that the present Gaelic Athletic Association is simply a rallying point for Irish nationalism. Nationalism in Ireland is multi-faceted and the Association has managed to transcend many of the tensions and divisions within it. The G.A.A. has reflected the country as a whole, sometimes nationalist, parts more nationalist than others, some parts with little nationalist tradition, but always distinctive. As the G.A.A. itself states:

> The Association is a national organisation which has as its basic aim
> the strengthening of National identity in a 32 county Ireland through
> the preservation and promotion of Gaelic games and pastimes.[13]

Although deeply embedded in Irish culture and being a bastion
of Irish identity, in the Republic of Ireland the G.A.A. and its
members often exist untouched by many of the considerations
which endure in Northern Ireland. In the north of Ireland in
particular, where the situation and context of everyday life is
affected to a greater of lesser degree by religious, cultural and
political cleavage, the Association continues to perform:

> a general and complex political function, as an advocate of Irish
> independence and national unity, as a symbol of Gaelic separateness
> and as an open forum for the allegiances of all factions of nationalist
> persuasion.[14]

Thus, the G.A.A. and its membership are viewed with deep
hostility by many in the unionist population. However, this also
has to be viewed in the context of the historical conflict between
'gael' and 'planter', a factor which has determined distinctions
throughout much of northern Irish life. Even where Nationalist
and Unionist, Catholic and Protestant share cultural forms, division
and conflict also have a role. Within soccer and rugby for example,
allegiances and participation are frequently informed by ethno-
religious and political factors. The G.A.A. in Ireland has historically
intertwined and become part of this larger depiction.

Some historical, political and journalistic observers have slated
the G.A.A., denying it a role in contributing positively to modern
Irish identities and arguing that it has failed to 'respond to the
forces of modernism and revisionism',[15] Such arguments frequently
posit political argument under the guise of revisionist academic
research, but they often also ignore the reality of experience and
informed perceptions, as well as undermine the role of
outstanding individuals and groups in the historical dialectic.
Although a unique sport amongst the Irish and their offspring,
many G.A.A. 'people' also participate and contribute beyond the
confines of the specifics attached to gaelic sports. Despite being
'peculiarly Irish', involvement with and support for the G.A.A.
cannot simply be taken as an indication of a parochial outlook.
Revisionism is essential in historical debate, but negates itself as
academic when carried in the guise of 'neutrality' only to be

sophistically construed as political and cultural opposition. Sclesinger makes the important point that:

> to assert that national cultures might, indeed, do, exist does not by any means exclude the reality of their being a transnational or global culture as well. We need to think in terms of the simultaneous interaction and parallelism of different cultural levels within given social formations. To insist upon 'either...or' makes for good polemics or political sloganeering but poor analysis.[16]

In Ireland, although historical circumstances has meant culture can also be politics in its broadest sense, and therefore also a means to make a political statement, the majority of G.A.A. members are not immediately concerned with political issues. The glories of sporting achievement predominate. In some parts of Ireland the G.A.A.s membership is politically conscious, and involvement with the Association is an underlying though varying, cultural and political statement. Nevertheless, the pursuit of human achievement, accomplished for individual, family or locale, is a major driving force for many gaelic enthusiasts. Within the G.A.A., ethnic origin, region, locale, religion, nationalism, politics, culture and even class, all within a context of 'Irishness', have and continue to make, significant contribution to gaelic sporting identities. Though few can detach themselves from the central tenets and symbols of the G.A.A., it can also be a variety of things to different people. It can be a way of life, a statement, a badge, whilst it can also be simply a game: just a game! Ultimately, gaelic sport is culture. For one of Ireland's most successful gaelic football players of the 1990s:

> There's nothing better than seeing the basic skills performed well...blocking, catching and kicking. The game in its purest form.[17]

Likewise for a prominent and successful hurling manager of the 1990s:

> Living in the present of Ireland rather than trying to live in the past. I find that bigotry disgraceful, and distasteful and disgusting'. I don't care which side its on. Nationalism is fine, but I'm living it. We're really living it.[18]

The Association has been faced with problems regarding the most recent 'nationalist' para-military campaign. This para-military campaign has been portrayed by much of the media and some politicians in both Ireland and Britain as encapsulating the essence of the Association as well as the ideals of Irish nationalism. As the media has frequently shaped the discussion of the Northern Ireland troubles around a question of nationalist violence, support for Irish nationalism is often viewed solely in this context. Therefore, people who are seen to support an Irish nationalist agenda, have become demonised and marginalised within Irish and British societies. There is a popular assumption that support for Irish independence and unity or, Irish nationalism, as well as criticism of Britain's role in Ireland, equates with support for or ambiguity towards violent atrocities. This is an assumption which is misinformed and superficial. It is also one which creates difficulty for the G.A.A. Although the Association can be characterised as patriotic and nationalist, it is inaccurate to view it as actively seeking the unity of the island. Such matters are left to politicians. Party or factional advantage or domination within the G.A.A. could prove to be its undoing. As 1900

Although political strength or intensity within a particular G.A.A. club might be significant in some areas, G.A.A. sports are pursued as sports, and the political dimension is more characterised as national and patriotic symbolism and tokenism. It is something which is intuitively part of the G.A.A., rather than the G.A.A. being part of it. For individuals and communities who would not continence armed struggle in the 'cause of Ireland', the G.A.A. is an agency for expression; a peaceful means to express their historic Irish identity which has been unable to escape, or has only partly emancipated itself from British domination and influence. Likewise, for many G.A.A. members, particularly those in the North, rule twenty-one which disbars members of the 'Crown Forces', from being members of the Association, is not a weapon, but a shield, a comfort, not an insult.[19]

Politics and Irish identity: Scotland

The politics of Irish independence and unity have long had resonance amongst the Irish abroad including the Irish diaspora in Scotland. Part of the legacy of a cultural and political assertion which refuses to submit to a perception of dominance and of anti-Irish expressions has, as referred to by Dr Douglas Hyde, been the inclination or custom to name a gaelic club after a recognised national, nationalist or patriotic hero. Many gaelic clubs have been named after Catholic parishes or Irish symbols, but a high proportion of clubs all over Ireland are called after an individual discerned in some way as having given their lives for the 'cause of Ireland'.

The Pre-match *Irish News,* Guinness sponsored souvenir paper, contained a half page of 'best wishes' for the County Tyrone team which was about to partake in the 1995 All-Ireland Final. All the county's famous clubs contributed. They included Coalisland Fianna, Tomas Clarke's, Pomeroy Plunketts, Galbally Pearses, Derrylaughan Kevin Barry's, Aughabrack O'Connell's, Drumragh Sarsfields, Kildress Wolfe Tones, Eoghain Rua Ui Neill, Ardboe O'Donovan, Cogher Eire Og: all names which have broadly defined 'nationalist' connotations. They include Tom Clarke, Joseph Plunkett and Padraic Pearse, three of the leaders of the 1916 Uprising, Wolfe Tone, a Protestant and the considered father of contemporary Irish republicanism, as well as Patrick Sarsfield, who led Irish armies against the Crown forces of King William in the 17th century.

Within many Irish immigrant communities in the early 20th century the practice of calling an organisation in memory of a perceived patriot was commonplace. For example, in Scotland, this reflected in the names of National Forresters friendly society branches. Kevin Barry (Edinburgh), Thomas Meaghar (Motherwell), Owen Roe O Neill (Greenock), Michael Davitt (Coatbridge), Charles Kickham (Glasgow), Young Ireland (Springburn) and Robert Emmet (Falkirk). During the early 20th century, other branches as well as additional Irish organisations such as the Gaelic League included Shamrock's and O Connell's, priests and Irish Saints as their branch names in Scotland. Such names were exclusively Irish and reflected a distinctive view of Ireland's history, particularly the conflictual aspects in relation to its near neighbour.

A number of gaelic clubs in Scotland have followed suit during the course of G.A.A. history. The first club in Scotland was of course Red Hugh O Neills founded in 1897. In the 1920s Patrick Sarsfield had two clubs named after him in Coatbridge and Greenock, the 1940s witnessed the Thomas Davis Club in Motherwell, Padraic Pearses and Fintan Lalors from Glasgow, Roger Casements in Clydebank and South O Hanlon's of Glasgow in the 1960s. In the late 1960s, violence and civil conflict again erupted in Ireland, on this occasion, almost solely confined to the North. With the revival of the G.A.A. in Scotland since the early 1980s, a number of clubs have emerged which have chosen names reflecting Ireland's troubled past. However, with the Northern Ireland conflict in the background, this has meant a tendentious journey for several clubs.

Pearse Harps, based at Pearse Park in the Cambuslang area of Glasgow, found itself nameless as the club was about to engage in its first competitive encounter during March 1985. Before the game a handful of the club's players met in the antiquated dressing rooms at the park and decided to link the new team with their home ground. Those who choose the name of the club were undoubtedly aware of the link also with the Rising in Dublin in 1916, Padraic Pearse being one of the prime movers in that event. Nonetheless, there was no conscious desire to connect the new club with an ideology of militant republicanism or even the current troubles. Pearse, a poet, educationalist and revolutionary, has also been commemorated during the 20th century alongside the evolution of the Irish state. This has included a main Railway station in Dublin being called after Pearse as well as his commemoration with the issuing of a special postage stamp on the centenary of his birth in 1979. Calling a gaelic football team after him continued the practice of numerous clubs' in Ireland and was for the new Pearse club, an imitation of a common cultural practice amongst many Irish people.

Founded in 1988 it would seem logical that in a city where another of the leaders of the Irish Rising of 1916 was born, a new Irish gaelic football team would consider naming the club after James Connolly. However, during the same period of the development of gaelic football in the area there was also a growth of Republican marches in the city and, the corresponding opposition of loyalists. The Republican organisation in the city was known as the James Connolly Society. As a result of these events, the name of James Connolly became synonymous with political and sectarian skirmishing which characterised these parades. Some of the first members of the new gaelic club, Dunedin Connolly's were associated with the James Connolly Society. However, after a few seasons the club became more influenced and indeed sustained by students from Ireland who attended courses in the local Edinburgh and Heriot Watt Universities. By the mid 1990s all of the club's original players had departed the football scene and the team was comprised almost entirely of young men originally from Ireland who worked and lived in Edinburgh, many with a number of financial institutions. Although in 1996 the club discussed changing the name of the team because of the players' awareness of 'outside' perceptions and suspicions, a decision was made to abide by the clubs name and hope that 'people could see beyond the prevalent sectarian perceptions which dominated'.[20]

Although Dundee Dalriada arose from a name which branches Ireland with Scotland, the first choice of the club's members was to name the team Dundee Fianna. This name evokes the Irish sagas of Cuchulain and others of a early stage of history on the island of Ireland. Na Fianna also translates as Fenians, the revolutionary body of Irishmen who engaged in military conflict with the British in Ireland during the mid to late 19th century. The first sponsors of the Dundee club, Tayprint, was reluctant to be seen to associate itself with such a label and the name was changed to Dalriada.

Another short lived team was that of Saltcoats Gaels. Based at Jack's Road in Saltcoats, and initially announced as The Invincibles, the club made their debut in senior football during season 1990. Naming the club after a tiny republican body which in 1892 assassinated T H Burke and Lord Frederick Cavendish, the newly appointed chief secretary for Ireland, the team's founder, John McCreadie, reacted to warnings of potential criticism by renaming the team.

One of the most significant Irish nationalist leaders of the late 19th century was Michael Davitt. Davitt was convicted of Fenian involvement in 1870, he was later to become a member of the Irish Republican Brotherhood, was imprisoned by the British, was an Irish Land Leaguer and subsequently became one of the foremost leaders of the Irish Home Rule movement. He had a deep influence on both the political ideas and activities of the 'Parnell era' in the late 19th century. Davitt was also closely involved with the Land League in north west Scotland. As far as some G.A.A. activists were concerned his name was thought worthy of a new club which began to be formed in Glasgow around 1995. However, despite a few active members and the involvement in a number of youths in gaelic football, coaching a competitive side failed to evolve in the same area of Glasgow which had produced the first gaelic athletic club in 1897.

In the mid 1980s, Coatbridge based gaelic football club Sands MacSwiney's developed from Pearse Harps in Cambuslang. For one former club member of Sands, its name was chosen to reflect the aspiration of an independent and united Ireland, 'just like the G.A.A. itself'. Although the initiators of the club were aware of the repercussions and labelling which may arise from its name, its founders were also convinced that it was erroneous to think that the name should be taken as an indication of support for any particular kind of nationalism, especially military. So why call a club after Bobby Sands and Terence MacSwiney?

Sands and MacSwiney are two of the most significant Republican figures in modern Irish history. Although sixty years separates their experiences both individuals encountered remarkably similar circumstances. Despite a variety of political opinion and historical interpretation characterising the Irish over the course of the seminal periods which surrounded the lives of Sands and MacSwiney's, a review of both individuals and the events which gave them a significant place in 20th century Irish history adds insight into the choice of such names on the part of many thousands of Gaelic Clubs since the founding of Red Hugh O Neills in Glasgow and Tuam Krugers in Galway in the late 19th century.

At the time of the Irish War of Independence, Terence MacSwiney was an educationalist, cultural activist, T.D. for mid-Cork, Lord Mayor of the City and Commandant of the Cork No. 1 Brigade of the Irish Republican Army, then fighting a popular campaign also known in Ireland as the 'Tan War'. In the two last posts, MacSwiney had replaced his friend and colleague Tomas MacCurtain, who was the victim of a premeditated execution by Crown forces in March 1920.[21] Costello believes that:

> Terence MacSwiney had shown himself to be a particularly dangerous man in the eyes of the British government. His multiplicity of Republican activities, together with the platform he occupied as lord mayor of Cork, had contributed greatly to the breakdown of the king's writ in Cork and in the country at large, which was now a hotbed of rebellion.[22]

As a result of opinion which viewed the Cork republican as dangerous, MacSwiney was arrested for possession of a R.I.C.

cipher code and other subversive documents. In protest at his imprisonment and British rule in Ireland, at a time when such men believed that the Irish Republic was a living reality, MacSwiney commenced a hunger strike. He believed that no British court should be able to pass judgement within an Irish jurisdiction. Costello opines:

> thus had began the battle of wills that would soon command worldwide attention, pitting a determined individual against the greatest empire of its time.[23]

MacSwiney was a particularly strong religious man. Six weeks after the commencement of his hunger strike, and contrary to his own expectations that his hunger strike could last so long, MacSwiney released a public statement:

> I attribute this to the spiritual strength which I receive from Daily Communion bringing me bodily strength assisted by a world of prayers, of which the intensity is so apparent. My comrades, who are fasting two days longer than I, are clearly sustained in like manner. I believe God has directly intervened to stay the tragedy for a while for a Divine purpose of his own: I believe he has intervened not solely for our sakes. We have laid our offering at his feet to be accepted or not, according to his Divine Will.[24]

Two of MacSwiney's sayings remain significant for modern day Irish nationalism: 'If I die I know the fruit will exceed the cost a thousand fold. The thought makes me happy. I thank God for it".[25] Also, 'this contest is one of endurance, and it is not those who inflict most, but those who can suffer most, who will conquer'.

During MacSwiney's hunger strike in Brixton Prison, both Cork and Tipperary G.A.A. called off most playing activities in a gesture of solidarity. The Munster hurling final was cancelled, a time when virtually the whole of Munster (apart from Waterford) was under military rule. After his death on the 25th October 1920, due to seventy-four days on Hunger Strike, Central council of the G.A.A. made a special announcement:

> Provincial Councils, County boards, League and Tournament Committees are hereby requested to make next Sunday, 31 October, a closed date all over Ireland so as to record the sympathy of the Gaelic Athletic Association with the Lady Mayoress of Cork in her great bereavement, our admiration for the Lord Mayor's heroic

sacrifice and to mark the Association's protest against the inhuman treatment meted out to the Lord Mayor of Cork by the British Government.[26]

Like Tom Ashe, who in 1917 had died as a result of forced feeding during a hunger strike, for many Irish people MacSwiney's death became a symbol of Irish resistance. Notably, Ashe was also a leading G.A.A figure in county Dublin before the Rising of 1916.

Tens of thousands of people attended MacSwiney's funeral along with thousands of Association members. Pope Benedict XV sent an Apostolic Blessing thus showing how deeply the perceived sacrifice had impressed beyond the shores of Ireland and Britain.[27] For supporters and sympathetic observers, MacSwiney embodied the ideal of sacrifice which has characterised many struggles compelled by a perception of injustice. Mahatma Ghandi in India and the suffragettes in Britain are two other such examples in which the British Government was also involved during the early 20th century.

Although not an active G.A.A. member, MacSwiney shared the ideals of many of the founders and supporters of the early Association. In similar style to people such as Archbishop Croke, Douglas Hyde and Patrick Nally, he spoke of:

> the hellish materialistic Power that has fastened itself on this our country by trickery and treachery; that had rooted one half of the people from the land and was stifling the soul of the other half; and had now stationed amongst us barracks and garrisons like the fang of some devilish ogre that we might not rush upon and struggle forever.[28]

In an open letter to the Cork Examiner, Bishop Cohalan of Cork stated that:

> I ask the favour of a little space to welcome home to the city he laboured for so zealously the hallowed remains of Lord Mayor Terence MacSwiney. For the moment, it might appear that he has died in defeat. This might be conceded if there were questions merely of the individual, but it is not true when the resolve of the nation is considered. Was Lord Edward Fitzgerald's death in vain? Was Robert Emmet's death in vain? Did Pearse and the other martyrs for the cause of Irish freedom die in vain? We are the weaker nation in the combat...Special questions such as the questions of the land, of local government, of housing, or education, for a time engage our whole attention. But periodically the memory of the martyr's death will

remind a young generation of the fundamental question of the freedom of Ireland...Terence MacSwiney's takes his place among the martyrs in the sacred cause of the freedom of Ireland...We bow in respect before his heroic sacrifice. We pray the Lord may have mercy on his soul.[29]

Originating from the pen of a well known anti-Republican, Cohalan's letter reflects the effect upon Ireland's struggle that perceived sacrifices of men such as MacSwiney has had. In such contexts, there can be a heightened awareness of Irish history amongst Irish people, which in turn often encourages G.A.A. members to name a club after an Irish patriot. Six decades after the death of MacSwiney a similar struggle again elevated the historical conflict involving Ireland and Britain in popular consciousness.

Like MacSwiney, Bobby Sands was a hunger striker. However, his death took place during the most recent phase of Ireland's troubles and for gaelic sports clubs whose members and founders have lived in the same era as Sands, selecting such a name could be construed as more subversive than that of using MacSwiney's who many people would be unaware of, and who may simply be viewed as another figure from the distant pantheons of Irish martyrdom.

Although not involved in G.A.A. matters to the extent of other hunger strikers like Kevin Lynch, who had captained a Derry minor team to all-Ireland hurling victory in the mid 1970s, Sands did play some gaelic football (as well as soccer) in the Belfast of his youth. Caught up in 'the Troubles', before joining the I.R.A. Sands had been stabbed in a sectarian assault and intimidated at gunpoint from his employment.[30] His confrontation with those he perceived as his oppressors met with his eventual arrest. By 1981 Bobby Sands was the Officer in Command of Republican prisoners in the H-Blocks of Long Kesh/The Maze Prison, having taken over from Brendan Hughes who had led a hunger strike in late 1980. In the wake of feeling deceived by the British Government in its dealings with the earlier hunger strike, and beginning on the 1st March of the following year, on the initiative of the prisoners Sands led another hunger strike. Sands thoughts on his own possible death resonates many of the deeper issues which have evolved during centuries of conflict.

My dear father and mother:

It is no joy to any one of us here to have to embark upon another hunger-strike. All of us realise and understand too well the consequences involved and torment endured by all the families but we have no alternative — ...Last Christmas was my ninth Christmas here in prison. I've lost because of it, including the wife I love and the son I love. Even so I would go back again tomorrow and fight because I'm not foolish, I'm not wild. I'm intelligent, responsible and hold ideals that generations have died for. I do not enjoy prison. I do not enjoy the thought of death...[31]

As Sands entered his hunger strike he embarked on maintaining a diary. His first entry read:

I am standing on the threshold of another trembling world. May God have mercy on my soul. My heart is very sore because I know that I have broken my poor mother's heart and my home is struck with unbearable anxiety. But I have considered all the arguments and tried every means to avoid what has become the unavoidable.[32]

Standing as an anti-H-Block candidate, in April 1981 Sands was elected Member of Parliament for Fermanagh/South Tyrone with over thirty thousand votes cast for him. G.A.A. matches all over the province were cancelled during the Hunger Strike:

The intensity of support for the prisoners and prisoners' rights, was expressed by individual clubs' throughout the area and votes of sympathy were unanimously passed on the death of the hunger strikers, many of whom were G.A.A. members'.[33]

As with the Catholic Church in much of Ireland, in the south the G.A.A. refused to become overtly embroiled in this aspect of the conflict, though its membership did participate to a greater or lesser extent. Many of the relevant statements of both hierarchies reflected a perception of the British Government as inhuman in its treatment of the striking prisoners and generally mishandling the conflict in the North. For Cardinal Tomas O Fiaich, the Catholic Primate of Ireland, the British government was in danger of incurring the wrath of the whole nationalist population if its rigid stance was not modified.[34]

After sixty-six days on hunger strike, Sands died on May 5th 1981. Around one hundred thousand people attended his funeral in Belfast: not in support of the campaign of the I.R.A., but within the complexity of Irish nationalism, to be seen as expressing solidarity with a perceived patriot who had reflected what they viewed as their centuries old suffering and struggle. Many people supported the current of Irish nationalism and many others supported those who were on hunger strike at the time. To view such expressions as support for armed struggle or for a campaign of terrorism is to misjudge Irish nationalism and indeed much of Irish history.

In most British political and journalistic circles as well as in popular ones, opinion was that Sands death was suicide: he was forced to die on the orders of the murderous, terrorist organisation to which he belonged. The *Daily Express* declared a common sentiment:

> Why do young men like Robert Sands commit suicide for such a cause? Because they follow darkness, believing it to be a romantic dream. Hatred is their goal.[35]

Outside of Britain and distinct from the Unionist community in Northern Ireland, perceptions of events like the Hunger Strike of 1981 and of the death of Bobby Sands were radically different from British views. In Poland, Lech Walesa considered Sands 'a great man who sacrificed his life for his struggle'. Walesa sent his deepest sympathy on behalf of Poland's Solidarity movement.[36] Around five thousand people demonstrated in Sands favour in Milan. The Portuguese Parliament observed a minutes silence and sixty MP's signed a document denouncing British intransigence during the Hunger Strike. In the European Parliament, the one hundred and twenty strong Socialist group sent a protest telegram to Margaret Thatcher. In the United States, dockers blocked British ships for twenty-four hours. The Indonesian Observer contained the headline, 'Bobby Sands, a Modern Martyr'. In India, Prime Minister, Indira Ghandi, sent a message to Margaret Thatcher attempting to intercede on Sands behalf. In the Indian Upper House, there were tributes to him 'of a kind normally reserved for dead head of states'.[37] Such views on Sands, the Hunger Strike and the conflict involving Ireland and Britain, are often at variance with dominant ones in Britain. In such perspectives, the views of many Irish also become less difficult to discern.

From an Irish nationalist perspective, it could be argued that Sands and MacSwiney personified the centuries old dreams of hundreds of dead patriots. Their vision also characterised many

G.A.A. founders and members throughout the late 19th and 20th centuries. Although the perspective amongst the Unionist community of Northern Ireland and amongst many people in Britain is often not only different, but fundamentally opposed to these ideals, calling a club after these individuals has been characteristic of not only the G.A.A., but for hundreds of years, numerous other Irish organisations; sporting, cultural and political.

For one member of the current Sands MacSwiney's Gaelic Football Club, he believes that:

> I've never known any of our members to be involved in politics of any kind — except for one who's a member of the local Labour Party. Gaelic football and promoting our Irish identity is what Sands is about.

Another member expressed the view that:

> As long as players want to play gaelic football and understand our links to Ireland, there's no reason for a problem. Some people have had the wrong impression regarding our team's name. There's no way I support violence.[38]

The experience of the Irish in Scotland during the 19th and 20th centuries has necessitated the use of a variety of strategies to deal with perceived hostility. For some immigrants and their offspring, this has resulted in a negation of their Irishness. Despite being a body of significant Irish identity, even in the context of the G.A.A. in Scotland, some members have attempted to conceal their own and the Association's Irishness. For some individuals within the Association, there has existed a belief that if it is arduous to exhibit Irish identity this reality should not be compounded by the use of patriotic names for clubs or any activity or voice which might be construed as 'political'.

The perceived hazards involved in using such names and even in being associated with the G.A.A. was reflected in the 1990s when Orange and Loyalist literature published articles depreciating Irish cultural activities in Scotland. Much of the comment and criticism related to the names of some gaelic clubs as well as in reference to the rules within the G.A.A. which bans British military personnel from membership.

> Loyalists may be surprised to learn that this Ayrshire coast town [Saltcoats] is the venue for frequent activity of an entirely different

nature. The town's Laigh Dyke Park frequently hosts contests between teams of the Gaelic Athletic Association (G.A.A.) which is, of course, the sporting wing of the I.R.A....[39]   *cyclists seen GAA as sporting wing of IRA*

Under the guise of culture a time bomb of sectarianism and political extremism is now in place in Scotland. It is hidden behind a spokescreen of sport and blarney...Rule 20 of the G.A.A. handbook prohibits any member of our fine Scottish regiments, the K.O.S.B., Gordons, Black Watch etc from playing this game in Pearse Park or anywhere else for that matter...The Irish have the same rights as every other group in this country to enjoy cultural activities...But it did seem strange for this promotion to be taking place in 1993, when the genuine Irish in Scotland seem to be fewer than they have ever been...[40]

The Invincibles Club in Saltcoats did change its name to one viewed as 'less prohibitive'. The Ayrshire team and its manager, County secretary John McCreadie, also experienced what they viewed as a degree of sectarianism because of the clubs presence on the gaelic scene. The club's football park and meeting place were noted in Loyalist literature with a view to it being subjected to pressure to desist from playing. As County secretary, McCreadie pursued a Scotland G.A.A. application to join the Scottish Sports Council in the early 1990s· such a membership potentially leading to grant applications and greater recognition. This was hampered, ostensibly because of a perceived lack of a Scotland wide spread within the G.A.A., despite clubs' in Edinburgh, Dundee, Ayrshire, Lanarkshire, Glasgow and Dumbarton. However, McCreadie, believes that the presence of a former police chief constable on the Council caused the application to be rejected on the basis of his interpretation of the G.A.A.s policy with regards members of   *Rule 21* the 'Crown forces'. When it transpired that such a rule had an historic and contemporary relevance in Ireland and that the Clan na Gael Club in Hamilton could in fact be contacted using the phone number of a police officer in a local station who played with the Clan na Gael Club, McCreadie believes some attitudes softened. A defence of the G.A.A. was also conducted by Glasgow M.P., Mike Watson, who met with the British Sports Council in response to his discovering the problems encountered by some of his local G.A.A. constituents. The G.A.A. was eventually advised that individual clubs could apply for funding. In all, the application took approximately thirty months to evolve to a stage where clubs could apply as individual bodies.[41]

Although less significant in media, cultural or political terms, as in Northern Ireland, the G.A.A. in Scotland has faced opposition. In the early 1990s a cross erected to the memory of Padraic Pearse at Pearse Park was vandalised and destroyed. The Glasgow field has also attracted the attentions of organisations such as the British National Party and Loyalist paramilitary support groups.[42] Such experiences have occasionally caused division within the G.A.A. in Scotland, manifest in debate at County Board meetings. The founding members of Sands MacSwiney's in Coatbridge experienced the internal politics of the G.A.A. in Scotland when shortly after the club's initiation a request for the new team to change its name was made on the part of some members of the County Board. The advice to the Sands management was that MacSwiney's could be retained but the use of the name of Sands would attract unwarranted and unwelcome attention from hostile elements. On this issue the Board were divided though most of the membership supported Sands in the naming of the club. Nonetheless, after initiating a minor set up in the early 1990s, part of Sands new management body relented to the hostile perceptions as well as negative hearsay and changed the name of its juvenile teams to Coatbridge Gaelic Boys Club, later to become Coatbridge Gaels.

Distinct even from the patriotic or political nature of the G.A.A., and although the G.A.A. in Scotland has traditionally been a forum for Irish identity, some members regard this Irishness in Scottish society as burdensome. Throughout the period of revival since the mid-1980s, representatives of Dumbarton's Saint Patrick's club continually stressed a perceived need to curtail and dilute displays of Irishness while emphasising Scottish identity.[43] This has been a recurring argument used by Eamon Cullen, founder of Saint Patrick's, who stated at the County's 1996 convention that, contrary to the origins and raison d'être of the Gaelic Athletic Association, 'the G.A.A. in Scotland did not exist to produce little Irishmen'.[44] Although these expressions represent a minority outlook within the G.A.A. in Scotland, such views are also a manifestation of some of the dilemmas faced by people of Irish antecedents who wish to preserve Irish identity.

[handwritten margin note: Some Irish thought they had to hid their origin to be accepted]

As reflected in research published elsewhere, there exists a perception amongst some Irish that to be accepted in Scotland, and as a mark of familial and community progress, there is a need to discard cultural and national identities which originate in Ireland.[45] Such a response has been part of the range of strategies used by the immigrant community in an effort to be viewed more positively and amiably. For some immigrants and their families this has also meant that a social, cultural and political image has to be constructed in which the final definition is one in which 'Scottish' is viewed as a more acceptable and confident self-definition as well as one more readily employed to describe from the outside or, by 'the other'. Adverse comment towards people in Scotland who maintain a Irish identity recurs frequently, in particular through the medium of journalism. Indeed, this is also an implication in the noted criticism of the G.A.A. and Irish culture in Scotland on the part of the Orange Institution.

The efforts of some Catholics to diminish Irishness within the immigrant community, as well as media comment which has been partial and has been impeded by frequent use of the term 'sectarianism' whenever ethno-religious identity is reported in Scotland, reflects in debate within the Catholic community concerning the merits or otherwise of the retention of Irishness. Reference has been made to a change in identity within elements of the Catholic press in Scotland during the 1930s.[46] Since this period of change there has been conflict regarding expressions of Irish identity on the part of Scottish born Irish. A number of Catholic newspapers have periodically criticised Catholics who express Irishness, especially if it is seen as being at the expense of Scottishness. After one perceived newspaper attack upon the Irish in Scotland,[47] a number of readers answered back:

[handwritten margin note: papers attacked Scottish of Irish origins who maintained links.]

> Not for a long time have I witnessed the heritage of possibly 90% of Catholics in Scotland being so overtly dismissed and disregarded, if not indeed attacked...Most of my own social experiences here in Scotland are still very much of an Irish kind.[48]

> How close one wants to stay to one's roots is of course a personal decision and the ethnic Irish certainly don't need any lectures on 'valuing Irish ancestry above a Scottish birth'. It is hardly the function of a Catholic paper nor indeed of the Church to tell people where their loyalties should lie. Too many people in the Church in Scotland are ashamed of, and want to hide our Irish ancestry, this is why we

127

never hear them decrying those of Italian or Polish descent who are not all that bothered about a Scottish birth either.[49]

Even amongst the supporters of Celtic Football Club, an institution with a strong Irish identity and supported in the main by people of Irish antecedents, there has been discord in terms of the heritage of the club as well as criticism of the predilection of many of its fans to 'be more Irish than Scottish'. Gallagher notes that 'working-class Catholics in particular find it difficult to relate to the symbols of Scottish nationhood'.[50] One example of this lack of affinity has traditionally been witnessed in how many Celtic supporters have not aligned themselves with the Scottish international side, and in the 1980s and 1990s, instead gave support to the Republic of Ireland's international football representatives.[51] Questions relating to Celtic fans' attachment to the Scottish international side were echoed in two Celtic pre-match programmes during 1991.

> It was a little sad some Celtic supporters, Scots born and bred, seemed completely non-plussed by Scotland's achievement [in reaching the European Championship Finals] and that a number of these people would have been happier to see the Republic of Ireland reach Sweden. This reflects on no-one. Certainly it is only right in view of Celtic's many ties with Ireland that supporters should feel an affinity with the Republic of Ireland and want them to do well, but surely this should not be in preference to the place of their birth. [52]

> If a Celtic fan wishes to support Scotland, Ireland or both then good luck to him/her…but the highs and lows of the Scottish side hold little interest for many of us. If we wish the Irish success then we're quite entitled to do so.[53]

Such debate as well as an hostility towards Irish identity in Scotland has a parallel with some attitudes towards Asian immigrants in English society. This was demonstrated in 1989 when ex-British Cabinet minister Norman Tebbit, demonstrated a comparable perspective suggesting a novel type of cricket test (or loyalty test). Asian immigrants integration could be tested by asking which cricket team they supported: England or Pakistan/India. He went on to suggest:

> that those who continue to cheer for India and Pakistan, are wanting in Britishness…that the only satisfactory way to be an Asian in Britain was to cease being Asian.[54]

The cricket test, in its form as a 'football test', has also been applied regularly by the Scottish/British press in the 1980s and 1990s as it became common for British born 2nd and 3rd generation Irish to represent and support the Republic of Ireland in international football. Critical comment, mainly regarding the immigrant identity of many members of the team, has characterised parts of the British media during this period.[55] The logic which underpins such an argument was exposed by a respected British journalist:

> the assertion that we are one people, has always been a lie used to justify the unjust dominance of one group (whites, Protestants or Anglo-Saxons, for example) over the society as a whole.[56]

Such cases reflect a widely held broad ideological and attitudinal position in parts of Scottish society where Irish matters are viewed with hostility. To be viewed as Irish, especially if one has been born in Scotland, frequently means that one has failed 'the loyalty test'. For example, although unrepresentative of all of Scots, the unacceptability of Irish-Catholics (particularly if born in Scotland) to the Orange community in Scotland, is one of the most perceptible contemporary manifestations of hostility towards the immigrant diaspora.

> Study the [Irish-Catholic] names of some of the 'Labour' candidates elected. What do Glasgow's Protestant clergymen think of this situation? What do the genuine patriots, in the SNP's rank-and-file, think about it?...and how do they relish the thought of their city — the birthplace too of so many famous Scots — being run by a bunch of Roman Catholics of immigrant Eirish stock (that's 'nationalism' not 'racialism') hardly outstanding for their talents, culture, or general education? Some Glasgow Roman Catholics may claim to be 'lapsed' Roman Catholics (who never criticise their Church), but they are never 'lapsed' Eirishmen! There isn't a Scoto-Eirishman in Scotland, a Lally, a Murphy, or a Gaffney, who is not Eirish under his skin. Scratch them and their Eirish bit comes out. That is why their priests are so committed to segregated schooling. To teach them 'history' with a Roman Catholic and Eirish slant. To pump into them whatever politics suits at the time and place. The children leave the Roman Catholic schools in this country semi-prepared or conditioned to vote Labour...[57]

Similar sentiments have frequently been expressed by some of the Reformed Churches in Scotland. In 1986, the Moderator of the

Free Church of Scotland addressed its annual Assembly. His speech included criticism of the Catholic and Irish nature of those of immigrant extraction:

> In 1755 there were no Roman Catholics in Glasgow, our largest city today. In 1786 there were about seventy and by 1830, they numbered 30,000, with 14,000 in Edinburgh...As the Irish came pouring into Scotland friction set in between Protestant and Roman Catholic working classes competing for work and housing...In our land the constitutional and institutional arrangements have led us to think that the land was Protestant...The 1918 Education Act incorporated all schools into the state system, but the State, in effect, had to buy the Catholic schools over...The short-sighted Presbyterians had their schools secularised and gained nothing. Educationally this meant that Scotland came to support a huge Irish Catholic educational ghetto, to its own future detriment...Today the Roman Catholic system is virtually triumphant in Scotland. Being allowed by its constitution to lie and cheat as long as its own ends are realised, its close organisation and its intelligence set-up has enabled it to infiltrate the whole educational framework of the land.[58]

Even where it is recognised that Scotland has been host to not only indigenous regional cultures as well as those contributed by migrants from English, Asian or Chinese backgrounds, the contribution made by the incoming Irish, certainly with reference to the west-central belt, is largely ignored throughout the education system as well as the media in Scottish society.[59] Reference to the Irish in Scotland is frequently conducted only through sectarian discourse.[60]

Given the growth of a secular society with its cultural and social implications, as well as the significant economic, social and political progress made by the offspring of the Irish in Scotland, particularly since the late 1960s, campaigns such as the Church of Scotland's in the inter-war years are unlikely to be repeated. Contemporary Scotland is more complex, and for some sections of the population, ethnic and religious identity becomes significant in fewer social and political situations and contexts than in the past. However, the publications and assertions of some Protestant Churches, organisations and individuals, and even from more secular sources, clearly remain anti-Irish and anti-Catholic. Comments from within some elements of Scotland's Catholic community regarding a lack of confidence, sometimes fear, in expressing and exhibiting Irishness, reflects some of the effects of anti-Irish aspects of society in Scotland and, Britain more generally. In its present more subtle and re-cycled form these remain a feature of modern society which continues to have an impact upon Irish identity in Scotland.[61]

One example of antagonism towards Irishness in Scotland, emerged from a writer to *The Herald* newspaper in 1990, when replying to a Celtic supporter's attack on Ranger's supposed sectarian playing staff policy. He wrote:

> I suggest that, when the flag of a foreign and frequently hostile state, whose constitution impudently claims sovereignty over part of the United Kingdom, and whose land and people the present pope has declared to be 'Mary's Dowry', no longer flies from the mast-head of 'Paradise', there may be, I say only may be, less 'bigoting' in the stands of Ibrox.[62]

The foreign state is the Republic of Ireland, Mary is the Virgin Mary and Paradise is the colloquial Celtic language for Celtic Park. Ibrox is the home of Glasgow Rangers Football Club. In such views, religion, politics and football are compounded.

As a result of the negative images excerted upon Irishness in Scotland/Britain since the 19th century, aspects of Irish identity have been influenced, even conditioned, by such discourses. As a result, the immigrant community has emerged as one which frequently deliberates its own identity.[63] The fluctuating but ultimately indeterminate nature of this identity, was summed up succinctly by one interviewee: 'I'm Scottish, though I've an Irish name. I'm more non-English. I am born in Scotland, but the blood that runs through me is Irish. If my background was black, I wouldn't be a half-caste. I'd be black'.[64]

The Irishness of the offspring of Scotland's Irish immigrant population is an area of dispute: an arena for social, cultural and political contestation. Many members of the G.A.A. in Scotland believe they have to tread a cautious path in their promotion of gaelic games as well as the Irish identity which often parallels gaelic sport. This has meant that hostility from outwith the community as well as from within are barriers to the sports advancement. With little acknowledgement to the Irishness of the community within the Scottish education system, academia or journalism, and with little recognition of the social, economic,

didnt see benefits
of Irish

cultural and political contribution its members have made to modern Scottish society, gaelic sports, like other manifestations of Irish identity in Scotland, exist within the confines of a situation defined originally within the context of the colonial relationship between Ireland and Britain.[65] In this context, in Scotland, members of the Irish diaspora who have retained and asserted Irish identity have long been engaged in attempts to promote Irishness in circumstances where there is a perception of hostility by their British/Scottish counterparts. This of course also has an historical context in relation to Ireland's centuries long domination by British influences, a domination which diminished Irish identity, the most obvious example being in the partial destruction of the use of the Irish language in Ireland.

Britain was men race against Be Irish

The rigours of a perceived struggle, to be seen as acceptable and not to be viewed with hostility by the wider society, is a history which distinguishes the Irish as well as the G.A.A. in Scotland. It is also one which has resonance with the origins and history of the Gaelic Athletic Association in Ireland, as well as having parallels with other elements of the Irish diaspora.

Notes

1. Dr Douglas Hyde, November 1892, from Purcell, 1982, p.236.
2. Padraig Uasal O Bogaigh, Uachtaran of the G.A.A., in Gaelic Athletic Association: a century of service, 1984–1994, 1984, p. 7.
3. Padraig O Fainin, in Gaelic Athletic Association: a century of service, 1984–1994, 1984, pp. 28–29.
4. Humphries, 1996, p. 5.
5. Ibid, p. 105.
6. Ibid, p. 129.
7. Flanagan, 1991, p. 46.
8. G.A.A grounds in Cork and Limerick were amongst the first to experience this in 1914.
9. Quinn. 1993, p. 91.
10. Scotland on Sunday, 7/12/97, p. 5.
11. Sugden and Bairner, in Allison, 1986, pp. 90–117.
12. Ibid.
13. The Gaelic Athletic Association: The Official Guide, Croke Park, Dublin, 1980.
14. Sugden and Bairner, in Allison, 1986, pp. 90–117.
15. For example see Cronin, 1996.

16. 1991, p. 305.
17. Quinn, 1993, p. 305.
18. Liam Griffin, manager of 1996 All-Ireland hurling champions Wexford, in Scotland on Sunday, 1/9/96, p. 21.
19. Humphries, 1996, p. 130.
20. Interview Dunedin Connolly's official.
21. Terence MacSwiney Diary, 9/9/02, MacSwiney Collection, from F J Costello, 1995, p. 117.
22. Ibid, p. 145.
23. Ibid, p. 150.
24. Ibid, p. 181.
25. Ibid, p. 150.
26. Purcell, 1982, p. 180.
27. Beresford, 1987, p. 18.
28. Costello, 1995, pp. 24–25.
29. Ibid, pp. 230–231.
30. Feehan, p. 76.
31. Ibid, pp. 116–117.
32. Feehan, 1984, p. 118.
33. Flanagan, 1991, pp. 55–56.
34. Irish News, 22/5/1981.
35. Feehan, 1984, p. 22.
36. Ibid, p. 21.
37. Dolan, Irish Post, 11/5/1991.
38. Interviews with Sands MacSwiney's members, June 1997.
39. Red Hand, a Scottish loyalist publication, issue 9, 1991.
40. Orange Torch, March, 1993.
41. Interview, John McCreadie.
42. G.A.A. members believe members of these groups smashed the Padraic Pearse memorial cross at Pearse Park in the early 1990s.
43. The use of the Irish national flag (which the G.A.A. requires to be flown at all games in Ireland and important games in Britain) as well as Irish marching bands on the occasions of championship finals were repeatedly a focus for criticism during the 1980s and 1990s on the part of Dumbarton's Saint Patrick's delegates at County Board meetings.
44. Eamon Cullen at minor County Board meeting and annual convention, both 1996.
45. See Bradley, 1995, chapter 6.
46. Ibid, chapter 5.
47. Scottish Catholic Observer, 19/10/1990.
48. Ibid, 2/11/1990.
49. Ibid, 16/11/1990.
50. Gallagher, 1987, p. 352.

51. Bradley, 1995.
52. Celtic match programme versus Dunfermline, 30/11/1991. Article written by Celtic View editor, Andrew Smith.
53. Celtic match programme versus St Mirren, 14/12/1991. Article written by Joe McHugh.
54. Quoted by Michael Ignatieff, Sunday Observer, 16/9/1990.
55. For example, see Phil MacGiollabhain's article, Irish Post, 27/3/1993.
56. Adam Lively, Sunday Observer, 22/7/1990.
57. Orange Torch 1984.
58. Moderators address to the Free Church Assembly, from Church Records, July/August 1986.
59. See essay by Robbie Robertson, Assistant director of the Scottish Consultative Council on the Curriculum, Daily Mail, 15/5/97.
60. See Bradley, 1995.
61. Ibid.
62. Dr B C Campbell, letter to Glasgow Herald, 6/5/1989.
63. This, in as much as the vast majority of Catholics in Scotland share a common background and often a common perception of many features of their identity. Of course, in an era of Americanisation, globalisation and with the pervasiveness of popular television and sport, they will also share many cultural, social and political features with other immigrant groups, as well as the non-immigrant or more indigenous population.
64. Interview with member of Celtic View staff, August 1994.
65. See Bradley, 1995.

29. *Charlie Quinn (wearing hat) and John Keaveney at the newly-purchased Eastfield Park in Glasgow, 1953.*

30. *Cois Tine, Glasgow, marking the Feast of St Brigid, 1978.*

31. Pearse Memorial Cross, Pearse Park.

32. Early Efforts to re-start hurling and Camogie in Glasgow, 1988.

strathclyde
irish festival
1989

Sunday 4th June
Espieside Park, Coatbridge
1.00 p.m.

Gaelic Football, Traditional Irish music and Irish dancing display.

St. Patrick's Hall,
Main St., Coatbridge
8.00 p.m.

Irish Folk nigh with "The Kells".
Admission - £3 (including food).

Monday 5th June
St. Mungo Club,
Gr. Western Rd., Glasgow
8.00 p.m.

Irish ballad session.
Admission — £2.50 (including food).

Tuesday 6th June
Lecture room 2., Third floor,
McCance Building,
Strathclyde University,
Richmond St. Glasgow
7.30 p.m.

Seminar on the Irish in Scotland. Invited speakers include, Dr. Tom Gallagher — Head of Peace Studies at Bradford University and Dr. James Treble — Strathclyde University History Department. Admission Free.

Wednesday 7th June
Glasgow Film Theatre,
Rose. St, Glasgow
3.30 p.m.

THE DAWNING — Set in revolutionary Ireland in 1920 this enjoyable period drama stars Anthony Hopkins, Jean Simmons and Trevor Howard. UK 1988 97mins.

St. Mathew's Hall,
South Crosshill Rd.,
Bishopbriggs
7.30 p.m.

Traditional Irish music concert with the Irish Minstrels branch of Comhalts Ceoltoiri Eireann. Admission — £2 Adults, £1 Children.

Thursday 8th June
Glasgow Film Theatre,
Rose St. Glasgow
6.00 p.m.

THE DAWNING

St. Bridget's Hall,
Swinton. Rd.
Baillieston
7.30 p.m.

Strathclyde Irish Festival Quiz competition final. Admission £1.

Friday 9th June
Govanhill Neighbourhood
Centre, Daisy St.,
Glasgow
8.00 p.m.

Gaelic League (Irish Language) workshops. Evening will include lecture on the history of the Gaelic League in Scotland, beginners guide to Irish Language and singing workshops. Co. Louth based singer and harpist, Carmel Boyle, will conclude the eveing with a selection of traditional songs and tunes. Admission Free.

Saturday 10th June
Glada Social Club
Westmoreland
Govanhill
Glasgow
10.30 a.m.

Traditional Irish set dancing workshop. Teachers, Michael Mulkerrin and Seamus O'Mealoid. Both from Co. Dublin. Admission — £2.

St. Bride's Hall,
Coursington. Rd.,
Motherwell
7.30 pm be
seated by 7.15p.m.

The St. Wilfrid's branch of Comhaltas Ceoltoiri Eireann, from Manchester, will perform "The day of the matchmaking". A comedy play about matchmaking in ancient Ireland. Followed by ceili dance and concert, with Carmel Boyle, the Johny Doherty and St. Wifrid's ceili bands. Admission £2.50 (Adults) £1.50 (children)

Sunday 11th June
Pearse Park
Eastfield
Cambuslang
12 00 p.m.

Day of sporting and cultural activity including set dancing competitions, Irish dancing displays, gaelic football, shinty versus hurling compromise rules game, and children's races. A number of live bands will appear, headed by the Seamus McGee showband, from Co. Donegal, and Carmel Boyle. Local folk and ceili bands will be there also. Stalls selling Irish produce and souvenirs will be an extra feature of the day. Admission £1. Children free.

Burnside Hotel,
East Kilbride Rd.,
Rutherglen
8.30 p.m.

Seamus McGee band appearing live. Limited tickets available.

Tickets for all events
are available from
Hobsons Newsagents,
8 Saltmarket, Glasgow
or
McCall's Newsagents,
Calder St.,
at Westmoreland St.
Glasgow

33. Programme for the Strathclye Irish Festival, 1989.

137

34. Glasgow's Lord Provost, Susan Baird, with Owen McAuley, a local Irish dancer, launching the 1990 Strathclyde Irish Festival during Glasgow's European reign as the City of Culture.

35. President of Ireland, Mary Robinson, is welcomed by local politicians on her visit to representatives of Glasgow's Irish organisations in 1992.

36. Members of Sands MacSwiney's G.F.C. welcome the 1993 All-Ireland Football winning coach, Mickey Moran, of Derry, and the Sam Maguire trophy to Coatbridge.

37. T P Murphy (International Workgroup) and G.A.A. President, Jack Bootham, at St Jude's Primary School, Barlanark, Glasgow, for the launch of the Coaching Pilot Scheme, 1994.

38. *Celtic Football Club. The primary focus and manifestation of 'Irishness' amongst the Irish dispora in Scotland* (Courtesy The Herald and Evening Times).

39. *Jimmy McHugh, Anne Doherty, Anne McHugh and Owen Kelly, founding members in the 1950s of the Irish Minstrels' Branch of Comhaltas Ceoltoiri Eireann, the first branch to be founded in Britain.*

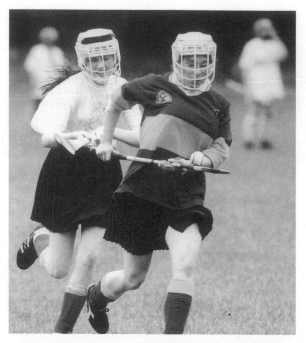

40. Tir Conail Harps v. Lochgilphead, shinty/camogie, 1996.

41. Paddy Gavigan, of Mulroy Gaels, receives the football championship trophy on the centenary of the founding of the first G.A.A. club in Glasgow. Molly Quinn and Owen Kelly make the presentation at Pearse Park in September, 1997.

CHAPTER 11

THE G.A.A., IRELAND
AND THE IRISH IN SCOTLAND

Culture is the ideas and attitudes of people: it is an indication of how we view things and it is a response to the environment in which we live.[1]

The search for distinctiveness and community

By the 1990s, the G.A.A. in Ireland had become a much changed organisation. Although remaining amateur, the clubs and the Association attracted major sponsorship as well as massive media coverage. Important for the gaelic sporting diaspora in Britain has been coverage of Irish sport by British television companies, but particularly by Channel 4, Sky Television and the Setanta satellite channel which in the mid 1990s covered annual activity in both hurling and football All-Ireland competitions. Training and coaching have become more intense and sophisticated and sports psychology also plays a role. Over two thousand clubs' and thousands more teams exist and many have their own grounds, pitches and clubhouses. Gaelic sport is part of the curriculum in Irish schools. The infra structure of the G.A.A. is constantly being updated and modernised. The headquarters of the G.A.A. in Dublin, Croke Park, is one of the best sports stadiums in Europe, with all the corporate and visitor facilities to which such stadiums have become accustomed.

For many Irish people, Ireland has acquired one of its historical aspirations: it has partly succeeded, in taking 'its place amongst the nations of the earth'.[2] For others too, the intensity, relevance and context of the historical Irish-British conflict has changed since the founding years of the G.A.A. The conflict is perceived differently by many Irish, north and south of the border, and these differences are reflected amongst the Irish diaspora. Irish nationalism has varied in response to a changing economic, social and political environment within which it exists. This links with the role of the G.A.A. which has also changed to become less important in the politics of the island. With regards Irish

143

nationalism, changes within that identity and ideology link with contemporary social and cultural theory which contends:

> nationalism is not fixed, but is a process contoured by the changing political, cultural and economic forces in specific social systems.[3]

Study of sporting institutions, activity and participation, has been well established as important to developing more credible and accurate assessments of society. In modern societies, it is virtually impossible for significant sports to exist without forming a relationship with other social and political institutions as well as mass movements.[4] Using the example of soccer, Finn has helped establish that many of the clubs' in present day Scotland have religious and political origins and roots.[5] Such evidence also shows that Celtic Football Club, an institution which evolved from and continues to draw the vast majority of its support from offspring of the Irish Catholic immigrant population in Scotland, is not unique, even in its particular Scottish context. Clubs such as Glasgow Rangers, Queens Park, Moffat, Larkhall Royal Albert and many others are shown by Finn to have been given birth within a context of religious or political backgrounds. Examples from other countries also reflect that sport, and soccer in particular, often have a socio-political, national or ethnic context which provides a basis for development and success, as well as a distinct rationale for existing.

Over the course of the 20th century, sport has contributed to war and peace, status and ideology, as well as art, health and, personal, community, ethnic and national relationships. In the latter part of the century, economics and wealth have had an increasingly significant impact on the direction and shape of modern sporting activity. Sport is largely inseparable from these features of human existence. Indeed, despite the often heard argument that 'sport and politics shouldn't mix', and notwithstanding sports often inherent physical and artistic qualities, sport is frequently not only social assertion, but politics by other means. That is not to say 'party political', but politics broadly defined as man temporarily producing winners and losers, as a forum to re-live, engage in and settle conflicts, discord and antagonisms, as well as raise consciousness and vitality in relation to the things which give meaning to peoples lives. Sport is intrinsically competitive, often between the competitors, but also frequently reflected amongst spectators. It is inherent to sports success that opposition as well as affinity and support develop. This revives Hoberman's belief that sport is 'a ready and flexible vehicle through which ideological associations can be reinforced'.[6]

Many examples of how sport is but an extension of relevant social and political features of everyday life can be found in numerous societies. In Spain, soccer has become synonymous with regional and ethnic identities. In the U.S.A. events in 1997 meant that in winning the U.S. Masters Tournament, negative reports of the experiences of black golfing hero, Tiger Woods, demonstrated to the world that racism does not simply take place in Holywood films and television dramas which have black ghettos as a part of their backdrop. Media reports of the experiences of Woods reflect that racism against blacks has been all pervading and continues to affect many areas of life in the U.S.A. Sport in the U.S.A reflects this reality. In a Scottish context, Jarvie and Walker believe that:

> sport and in particular, football, is a central arena for the expression of a range of Scottish national identities in both domestic and international contexts.[7]

Although the G.A.A. can be viewed as being unusual in a sporting context, it is hardly unique. The G.A.A. is but one example of a sporting body or vehicle which has its origins, links and its very meaning, closely associated with culture, nationalism and patriotism. The case of the G.A.A. has a number of parallels and close relations in other countries. Sport is a two way relationship with individual, community and national identity. Such associations are intrinsic to the Gaelic Athletic Association: a body which remains uniquely amateur. Perceptions of the G.A.A. vary across Ireland though the links between sport, nationalism and religion in Ireland remain significant and, are particularly strong in Northern Ireland where the Association is broadly nationalist, but factionally neutral. Although context and circumstances vary enormously between Ireland and Scotland, the G.A.A. is an important aspect of Irish identity among a section of the Irish community in Scotland in the west of the country. The G.A.A. promotes a sense of Irishness, both in its Irish and diasporic contexts. This sense of Irishness has political, cultural, sporting and communal aspects. These attributes can be singular and

SPORT, CULTURE, POLITICS AND SCOTTISH SOCIETY

collective and they can fluctuate, becoming circumstantial, temporary, or life long characteristics. Although many immigrants to Scotland originated from the southern half of Ireland where gaelic sports had become steadily better organised over the course of the late 19th and early 20th centuries, much of this phase of immigration took place before or during effective organising on the part of the G.A.A. in Ireland. These immigrants also entered a hostile environment where giving service to gaelic sports was difficult. Eventually, most immigrants came from Ulster and Conaught, where organised gaelic activities was often weak and where the Gaelic Athletic Association took many years to become established, taking until the 1930s in the province of Ulster before making an impact. conflict hindered its success

De Burca notes, that in 1889 many Ulster counties either did not have a functioning Association or were severely weak; in Monaghan, Derry, Antrim and Down insufficient clubs existed to form a county committee, whilst in Donegal, Fermanagh and Tyrone, there is little if any record of activity. By 1891, there was not a single club in Louth, Monaghan and Tyrone, whilst Mayo had only three and Clare one.[8] This must also be viewed in the context of the overall Association being inchoate. Again, during the troubled times of the Parnell era, the First World war, 1916 and the Irish War of Independence as well as during the period of the Irish Civil War, pastimes and cultural activities were negatively affected. In particular, counties where many G.A.A. activists were also volunteers with the nationalist movement often became athletically weak, as individuals and communities had little time to pursue recreational activities. By March 1915 for example, both gaelic codes had almost died out due to activity with the volunteer movement.[9]

Although it remains an aspect of Irish culture and Irish identity in Scotland, the conditions which gave rise to and sustained the Association in Ireland were not replicated in Scotland. Some conditions were closely related and were fed by similar historical factors, but Irish life outside of Ireland was also a differing experience. Even in the 1990s in the U.S.A., although having some vibrancy where Irish immigrants reside in large numbers, the G.A.A. also encounters difficulty in being viewed as a primary focus of Irish identity.

146

Since American-born Irish have traditionally shown little interest in the games of their fathers, the G.A.A. in America has always depended upon Irish immigrants to keep the games alive…As a matter of fact, were it not for Irish students who come to America during the Summer to work and line up with G.A.A. teams in various cities, the games of the Gael would be for all intents and purposes dead in many cities.[10]

Many of the things which today give life to the G.A.A. in Ireland, especially a sense of identity in the shape of parishes and counties, local tradition, history and bloodlines, added to coaching as a part of the modern educational curriculum, do not exist in Scotland. The sociology of gaelic sports which exists in Ireland does not constitute any real influence amongst the diaspora. In its island of Ireland context, for Humphries:

That the Gaelic Athletic Association succeeded at all is due to the manner in which the fare it offered fitted perfectly within the culture, rituals and aspirations of our society. On an island where native culture had for centuries been subordinated to political imperatives, the games became a passionate and rugged expression of a people's soul. When all other forms of Irishness had been stamped out, the spirit burst out of captivity in the form of play.[11]

Chairman of the London County Board in the early 1980s, F Shechan, believed the role of the G.A.A. to be extremely important with regards matters Irish in Britain. Although underestimating other social agents as well as other Irish identities, Sheehan captured some of the essence of the Association abroad on stating that:

The G.A.A. has its outpost in London for over eighty years kept going by Irishmen who valued at its true value and worth this great link with home. Today it is strong and flourishing just as the parent body is. In other parts of England too there are G.A.A. strongholds…Their simple purpose is to provide Irishmen and their sons with a means of expressing their individuality, of keeping alive that incredibly valuable work of nationality. Those who turn away from such an opportunity will soon be lost in the crowd, nonentities, without anything to distinguish them.[12]

Humphries second assessment seems to get closer to the Irish in Scotland experience:

> The culture of gaelic games has been built upon the Irish need for collective self-expression, the desperate hankering after something indigenous and Irish in a world which formally repressed such forms of articulation, a world which has become increasingly homogenised…Our distinctiveness no longer shames us.[13]

In Scotland, over the course of the late 19th and 20th centuries, a sporting form developed within the Irish immigrant community which was already a growing sports activity in Scotland and, which was quite distinct from the gaelic revival in Ireland: that is, the emergence of Celtic Football Club. At the time of the founding of Celtic in 1887/88, a majority of Catholics in west-central Scotland were from Ireland and the words Catholic and Irish were interchangeable. All the club's founders were expatriate Irishmen or of Irish antecedents and the new club's support was drawn largely from the swelling Irish community in Glasgow. The donations to charity frequently included some to Irish causes such as the Evicted Tenant's Fund, then an important aspect of Irish nationalist politics. Off the field, the national question was of crucial importance to Celtic's founders as it was to many in the immigrant community. Club officials, players and supporters alike, were often involved in politics; supporting Irish Home Rule, campaigning for the release of Irish political prisoners, opposing what they viewed as British imperialism in the Boer War and South Africa and supporting the contentious petition for Catholic schools to be maintained within the state system.

In a number of countries, football often has a broader ethnic and political resonance. For example, Spain has been one of the most significant examples of this feature of football. In northern Spain, the Catalan football club Barcelona, and the Basque Athletico Bilbao, have respectively become symbols for Catalan and Basque identity. One observer recounted how a woman told him of Barcelona Football Club:

> I detest football, but Barca is more than football. In the bad days, when we had nothing else, Barca meant Catalonia. People used to go to the stadium just to speak Catalan.[14]

In Scotland, soccer has become one of the most obvious of mediums for Irish identity. In similar fashion to clubs in Spain, Celtic Football Club possess a cultural, religious and political identity. Despite the G.A.A.s historic antagonism towards non-Irish

148

sports, Celtic Football Club's identity has similar features to that of the G.A.A.s. This, in as much that the club draws mainly on the Irish in Scotland and these members of the diaspora have become amongst the foremost of conveyors of Irishness in Scotland. This links with the G.A.A. as a chief conveyor of Irish identity in Ireland.[15]

During the 19th and 20th centuries, Irish immigrants and their offspring in Scotland encountered much opposition.[16] For the most part, hostility revolved around the religious, national and often the political character of the immigrants. In the face of antipathy shown to Irish immigrants, expressions of Irishness have often been problematic for that community. For many Catholics, football, and Celtic in particular, has provided an environment in which to make known otherwise repressed or unarticulated political attitudes, cultural affinities, national allegiances and prejudices.

football + celtic could express their Irishness in a non prob environment

Although historically an Irish club, Celtic's involvement in Scottish football also allowed for the participation of the immigrant Catholic community in a popular facet of the larger society. Football and Celtic became avenues for interaction and integration with the host community, despite the ethnic competitiveness of the game itself. For many members of the consciously Irish Catholic community,[17] or for those members of the immigrant community who retain a sense of 'Irishness', Celtic is the greatest single 'ethno-cultural focus' because it provides the social setting and process through which the community's sense of its own identity and difference from the indigenous community is sustained in and through a set of symbolic processes and representations. In becoming a focus for displaying Irishness Celtic has also become a unique football club in Scotland. Many emotions, sentiments and passions which might have been displayed elsewhere, or indeed were diminished in other contexts, became central to the character of the Celtic support. For many Irish immigrants in Scotland, supporting Celtic has been, 'a powerful strategy of identity building'.[18]

For many Catholics in Scotland, and in a similar fashion to Raynot's description of Barcelona Football Club being a vehicle for Catalan identity in Spain, Celtic have become a metaphor for aspects of the Irish and Catholic immigrant tradition.[19] In Scotland, football is bound up with the process of individual socialisation

149

and community construction. The history of Irish-British relations has meant that for the Irish in Scotland, as well as for those of an anti-Catholic and anti-Irish disposition, Celtic Football Club has emerged as a definition of Irishness itself.

For the G.A.A. in Scotland, the paradox which emerges from this situation is that a club, playing a sport marginalised and for so long banned by the gaelic authorities in Ireland and amongst the gaelic fraternity abroad, has for over one hundred years been the primary alternative vehicle for Irish identity in Scotland. With many Famine immigrants in Scotland being present before the founding of the G.A.A., with others immigrating during the first decades of the G.A.A.'s existence in Ireland and therefore before the organisation had become fully established, with many more immigrating from areas of Ulster and Conaught, where the Association was for a number of decades either poorly constituted or did not exist, soccer, largely within the context of Celtic Football Club, has attracted the energies and emotions of the Irish in Scotland.[20] Although Irishness is the principal identity of Celtic Football Club and its support, this has been to the dismay of some traditionalists amongst the G.A.A. in Scotland. Certainly, it may be argued that Celtic have been over dominant in terms of Irishness, so much so that other Irish bodies and organisations have suffered numerically and in terms of loyalty, affinity and expression. However, Celtic Football Club has also allowed for the maintenance and expression of Irish identity in often unfavourable circumstances. Over the course of the latter half of the 20th century, the maintenance of Irish identity through Celtic Football Club by many of the offspring of the Irish, has been a factor allowing for the re-emergence of gaelic football in Scotland. Indeed, in 1997 a significant number of G.A.A. members in Scotland, including several members of the County Board, were season ticket holders at Celtic F.C. However, while 1984 was a year of celebration for one hundred years of G.A.A. history, for the Irish and their offspring in Scotland the most important facet of their identity — Celtic, runners-up in the league to Dundee United, lost the Scottish Cup Final to Aberdeen. The match was attended by 59,000 and watched by millions as the game was televised live by both ITV and BBC. Less relevant for most the diaspora in Scotland, in 1984 Kerry won the All-Ireland football title and Cork defeated Offaly in the hurling final, both played at

150

Croke Park, Dublin. The important centenary for most of the Irish in Scotland was that of 1987/88 which celebrated the founding of Celtic Football Club.

Nonetheless, although a comparatively weak organisation, the history of the G.A.A. in Scottish society reflects that it has been an important focus of Irish identity for some of the diaspora. Although many of the Association's members have traditionally been a politically conscious grouping, the crucial factor in the involvement of most Irish in Scotland in the G.A.A., particularly those second and third generation, has been in viewing gaelic sport as a channel and vehicle for Irishness. Since 1984, the G.A.A. in Scotland has played a small, but notable role in maintaining and introducing ideas and images of Irishness amongst those with Irish antecedents in Scotland. For some activists, it provides an authentic, incontestable manifestation of their Irishness.

> Those who play Gaelic games and organise its activities see in the G.A.A a means of consolidating our Irish identity. The games to them are more than games...[21]

As in Ireland, gaelic games for G.A.A. enthusiasts in Scotland:

> ...epitomise the spirit and the personality and the character of the Irish more than anything...[22]

As with the example of Sam Maguire's life in Britain early in the 20th century, for many G.A.A. activists in Ireland and amongst its diaspora, their's is a cultural and ideological commitment to 'the promotion of a national identity'.[23]

The organisation of sport and its functions to society are important. In addition, the purpose of individual involvement in a specific cultural context, that is, in Scotland, has been primary in linking current G.A.A. activists in Scotland (and amongst the Irish diaspora generally) with the Association in Ireland: this in a frame of reference which invokes its early years. The myths of descent, historical memories, territorial association with Ireland, religion and a sense of solidarity, provides many G.A.A. activists in Scotland with their cultural and sporting motives. Ethnic and national consciousness is maintained through the G.A.A.. With three quarters of a million adults in membership within Ireland and the diaspora, thousands of children and many more people tied simply by emotion or occasional experience, the G.A.A. forms an important dimension of the Irish 'family' or diaspora, in addition to old and new conceptions of Irish identity. It also helps gives 'Irishness' a heterogeneous quality and outlook. As in Ireland, the G.A.A. in Scotland contributes to a distinctive ethnic identity. This distinctiveness is a primary reason for the survival of the Association in Scotland as well as the rationale and motivation for those who maintain its existence as a valuable dimension of Irish identity. The G.A.A. in Scotland provides an organisational locale for the idea of a common descent, a shared history in Ireland and common experience in Scotland. It provides for a concrete link with the country of birth or origin. It is both an expression of diversity and a symbol of identity.

Historically and in its contemporary setting, the culturally active and conscientious element within its membership have been primarily concerned with reawakening elements of the diaspora in Scotland to their Irish heritage. In this sense, the G.A.A. is viewed as a celebration of Irishness in a situation where many people of Irish origins have seen themselves, and their previous generations, as being compelled to seeing Irishness in a negative light.

Allison notes that:

> sport can be the object of great emotion and that the sentiments which surround it are not necessarily neutral in respect of politics or, even if neutral, certainly not inert.[24]

As with other elements of the immigrant diaspora, strong feelings often exist within the G.A.A. in Scotland with regards conflict in the north of Ireland, while it is also believed that popular British perceptions of the problem habitually negates political debate. The links between perceptions of sectarianism in both west central Scotland and Northern Ireland further means that the promotion of gaelic games has to be achieved within the context of ethno-religious cleavage.

Distinct from politics and culture, as in Ireland, much gaelic activity in Scotland is concerned with matches to be arranged, providing transport, coaching activities, methods of raising necessary finances and specifically in Scotland, with a lack of referees. Throughout the period since 1984, many clubs have struggled to meet fixtures and to maintain a cohesive and competitive club unit. Since the organisations most recent revival in Scotland many individuals have been lost to the G.A.A. and a number of clubs' have demised due to lack of leadership, the loss of significant players or even of difficulties in fielding enough players on a regular basis. By 1997, a consensus existed amongst gaelic activists in Scotland that lacking financial succour, coaching expertise, practical and urgent assistance from headquarters at Croke Park, progress made by the G.A.A. in Scotland since 1984 might be forfeited: so much so that gaelic sports in Scotland was at a juncture where it could once again demise. Ironically, as the G.A.A. in Scotland has steadily raised its playing standards during the 1990s, many players have faded from football activities due to the increasing demands of more rigorous training and competition. Many such players, attracted to gaelic football because of its Irishness, have been unable to sustain the athleticness or the required improvement in skills as the game has progressed. However, at a time when many sports, which depend almost entirely on their participative elements, appear to be encountering difficulty due to the pressures of modern lifestyles, it is often the case that it is the Irish nature of gaelic sport which helps maintain its life in Scotland. Absent of images of community and a sense of identity, culture and heritage, the G.A.A. in Scotland would not exist one hundred years after the founding of the first club in Glasgow.

Though many individuals also departed gaelic sport during the 1980s and 1990s, they have also experienced and contributed to gaelic games and therefore, to the expression of Irish cultural identity in Scotland. Clubs such as Sands MacSwiney's in Coatbridge used around 150 players during a ten year period since its founding in 1986/87: around 30–40% immigrants to Scotland or third level students from Ireland based at Scottish universities. The rest of the Coatbridge club consisted almost wholly of players born in Scotland of Irish antecedents. Similarly, Paisley Gaels included Irish born players working or studying in Scotland along with many Scottish born players whose roots lie in a variety of locations in Ireland. Like Mulroy Gaels in Glasgow, the current Tir Conail Harps club with approximately 150 to 200 members, almost all of whom are 2nd, 3rd and 4th generation Irish youngsters in their teenage years, have significant links with Donegal. Added to these figures are those who have participated with now defunct teams' as well as the many hundreds of primary level schoolchildren, boys and girls who Shotts Gaels, St Patricks, Sands MacSwiney's, Beltane Shamrock's and Tir Conail Harps have introduced to gaelic games in the 1990s. By 1997, since the beginning of the revival of the Gaelic Athletic Association in Glasgow, approximately five thousand individuals experienced playing gaelic sports in Scotland, the majority of whom were born in Scotland of Irish forebears.

Despite being an historically small organisation in Scotland and, although largely peripheral to the Irishness of the vast majority of those of the immigrant diaspora in Scottish society, the G.A.A. and gaelic sports have provided an important expression of Irishness over one hundred years. As assertions of Irish identity in Scotland have expanded and become increasingly manifest in the 1980s and 1990s, the G.A.A. contains the potential to develop and become more important to the future history of the Irish in Scotland.

Notes

1. Adams, 1986, p. 137.
2. See Kee, 1976, p. 168, for quotation of Robert Emmet before his execution in 1803: '...When my country takes its place among the nations of the earth, then and not till then, let my epitaph be written'.
3. Reid, 1997, pp. 147–155.
4. Flanagan, 1991, p. 27.
5. See Finn, 1991.
6. Sugden and Bairner, 1993, p. 10.
7. Quoted in Boyle and Hayes, 1996, pp. 549–564.
8. de Burca, 1980, p. 58.
9. Ibid: p. 124.
10. Patrick Hennessy, in Gaelic Athletic Association: a century of service, 1984–1984, 1984, p. 79).
11. Humphries, 1992, p. 2.
12. Sheehan, May 1992 from Gallagher, 1993.
13. Humphries, 1996, p. 3.
14. Allison, 1986, pp. 2–3.
15. See Bradley, 1996.
16. See Handley 1964 and Gallagher, 1987.
17. There are of course a number of conceptual problems when viewing the Irish in Scotland. For example, the significant number

of marriages across communities invariably affects this concept. However, for many, particularly in the towns and areas of the west of Scotland, where there are meaningful numbers (almost all who are of the Catholic faith) who owe their descent to Irish born parents, grandparents and great grandparents, 'Irishness' is a clearly distinguishable culture and identity.

18. Rokkan and Urwin, 1983, p. 89.
19. Jay Raynor, The Independent on Sunday, 28/6/1992.
20. During the late 19th and early 20th centuries, other Irish football clubs' also existed in Scotland: Edinburgh's Hibernian, and Dundee's Dundee Harp (later to become Dundee United) surviving beyond their early difficulties. Nonetheless, Celtic F.C. remain the only club which can be considered in any way Irish in contemporary Scottish, indeed, British, society. See Bradley, 1996 (c).
21. G.A.A. Handbook, 1992.
22. Quoted by Liz Howard, Tipperary County Board, on Shinty: Sport of the Gael, BBC Scotland (television), 1993.
23. The Sam Maguire Cup, 1986.
24 Allison, 1986, pp. 1–26.

APPENDIX 1

Table A1.1
Football Club Championship Winners 1985–1997

Clubs which have won the County Board of Scotland Championship (formally Glasgow Championship) since the revival in 1984 (beaten finalists in brackets):

1985	Clan na Gael, Hamilton	(Mulroy Gaels)
1986	St Patrick's, Dumbarton	(Mulroy Gaels)
1987	St Patrick's, Dumbarton	(Sands MacSwiney's)
1988	Beltane Shamrock's, Wishaw	(Mulroy Gaels)
1989	Mulroy Gaels, Glasgow	(Sands MacSwiney's)
1990	Sands MacSwiney's, Coatbridge	(Mulroy Gaels)
1991	Sands MacSwiney's, Coatbridge	(Dundee Dalriada)
1992	Dundee Dalriada, Dundee	(Mulroy Gaels
1993	Dundee Dalriada, Dundee	(St Patrick's)
1994	Dunedin Connolly's, Edinburgh	(Dundee Dalriada)
1995	Mulroy Gaels, Glasgow	(St Patrick's)
1996	St Patrick's, Dumbarton	(Sands MacSwiney's)
1997	Mulroy Gaels, Glasgow	(St Patrick's)

APPENDIX 2

LIST OF MEMBER CLUBS: COUNTY BOARD OF GLASGOW/SCOTLAND 1984–97

Ayrshire Gaels, Saltcoats (1989–1990)

The wider cultural pursuits of Irish dancing brought into being the Saltcoats club, formally known as 'The Invincibles'. Following the fortunes of his daughters participation with the Setanta School of Irish Dancing, John McCreadie began socialising in circles frequented by existing members of the G.A.A. The decision to begin a club took place at a St Patrick's night in 1989, the team making its competitive debut the following year.

McCreadie, whose forebears came to Scotland from Antrim and Dublin, along with his cousin, John Toal, Eamon Rankin (Dublin), Noel Hughes (Leix) and Michael McLaughlin (Donegal), gave birth to the new team. Noel Hughes also made his mark as a player with the side along with his sons, Joe and Noel. The playing of Irish born team members was finally made up by Joe Tevenan (Dublin) and Joe Duffy (Donegal) as well as Tony Keane, a Sacred Heart Father from Dublin, based at his orders house in Kilwinning. On the whole, Saltcoats consisted mainly of Scottish born Irish as well as a few players who had no Irish connections, including importantly for McCreadie, around four or five non-Catholics.

The Ayrshire senior team lasted for one year whilst the minor set up lasted for around eighteen months. The main reason for the dissolution of the club was the onset of Sunday afternoon live televised soccer. With a majority of Gaels players also Celtic soccer supporters, football matches on Sunday's involving the Glasgow Club steadily eroded attendances at matches on Sundays.

Beltane Shamrock's, Wishaw (1986–1996)

Leading on from his success in Hamilton, Eamonn Sweeney inaugurated another club based around his new parish of St Aidan's, Wishaw, which was called after a local area in the town.

By the end of 1986 Wishaw played a few competitive matches while in 1987 they took part in all competitions.

Father Sweeney provided the Shamrock's with most of its direction. Sweeney's efforts to play and participate to the full reflected his love of the game. It was not unknown for Sweeney to serve 1.45pm Sunday Mass as Catholic chaplain at Law Hospital in Wishaw, then dash to play a game at 3.00pm, often wearing a football strip over his priestly garb, and often to places as far afield as Dumbarton and Edinburgh.

With Sweeney being the club's only Irish born player, and with ex-professional footballer Eric Rooney training the team, Beltane experienced their most successful period during their first season. Players Derek McStay, cousin of the famous Celtic soccer player Paul, Tom Delaney, Paul Toner, Billy Williamson, Tony Hogan, Jim Cusack and James Connolly, as well as parishioner Brian Brawley, assisted the St Aidan's curate, in reaching the Championship final of 1987. Playing the match at Wishaw Sports Centre, Shamrock's found themselves ten points down with five minutes remaining. The game turned around when the Wishaw side drew level to force extra time, subsequently winning convincingly due to superior fitness.

Eamonn Sweeney learned a number of lessons concerning the demise of his previous club in Hamilton. He recognised difficulties relating to player strength, training and finance with most gaelic clubs. He also believed that he had to inculcate a sense of affinity with gaelic sports in Ireland. Despite his best efforts, as well as those of Brawley and Andy Smith, and aside from a strong bank balance in place, Beltane Shamrock's folded after Sweeney left to become parish priest of St Michaels Moodiesburn, to east of Glasgow. Having struggled to field fifteen players for their first match of the season in Coatbridge, Beltane failed to field for the rest of the year. By 1997, it was officially announced that the club had demised.

Clann na Gael, Hamilton (1985–1987)

The driving force behind Gaelic football activities in the 1980s was Ballycroy Mayo priest, Eamonn Sweeney. During his ministry as a curate in St Ninian's Hamilton, Father Sweeney founded a local club to participate in the new Glasgow football league inaugurated in 1985. Matches were played at nearby Strathclyde Park were the pitch was named Loftus Park, after the then president of the G.A.A. in Ireland Sweeney's fellow Mayoman, Mick Loftus.

Made up almost entirely of local players recruited from his parish and nearby Holy Cross School, once again Clan na Gael proved the Scottish born Irish could excel at gaelic football. In its first season, Hamilton won its way to the Championship final to become victors in the first such competition held in Scotland for a generation. The Hamilton team celebrated its win with a trip to play in Ireland in September 1995. Challenge matches were held in Achill Island and Dublin whilst the latter location also witnessed the visitors from Scotland attend the All-Ireland final between Kerry and Dublin. Orla O Hanrahan, third secretary at the Irish Embassy in London, and Tom Walsh, well known Irish cultural activist from Liverpool, presented the Championship winning trophy to Hamilton at the end of the year. The involvement of such figures reflected the growing profile of the game in Scotland by 1985.

Added to his gaelic football activities Father Sweeney encouraged a number of gaelic clubs as well as Catholic parishes to participate in B & I Ferries sponsored 'Its a Knock-out' Festivals of 1985. Clan na Gael won the Scottish regional competition to lose in the finals held at Mossney Holiday Camp in County Louth. During this period the Hamilton team was well served by such as Paul Gallacher, Mick Cassidy (Mayo) and Kevin Brady.

Despite success, Clan na Gael failed to maintain their status as an active club on the departure of Father Sweeney for a new parish in Wishaw, Lanarkshire. Individuals such as Pat McFadden and Brian Molloy attempted to keep the club active, but by 1987 the club was extinct.

Coatbridge Gaels, (1991–)

Formed originally as Sands MacSwiney's Boys Club, members of Sands realised the future of gaelic sports depended not on the use of students from Ireland, but on the development of a local youth policy. Advertising in nearby schools and Catholic Churches, enough interest was generated to introduce hundreds of youngsters to the game during the early 1990s.

Coached in the main by senior players Peter Elliott and Eddie O Neil, and latterly by Stephen Traquair and Pat McHugh, Coatbridge Gaels experienced a challenge with numerous difficulties in sustaining a vibrant club. However, the club did entertain teams from Ireland and visited Skerries in County Dublin as well as Maghera, County Derry. By 1996/97 a number of players who has been introduced to the game in the early 1990s began to break into the Sands MacSwiney's team.

Cuchulain's, Glasgow (1992–1993)

This short lived club was set by Tommy Doherty whose family originated in Dungloe, County Donegal. Doherty's son was involved with the ailing Pearse Harps team when he decided to give birth to another club. Tommy Main and John Nally of the County Board along with Rory Campbell, whose sons also played with Pearse Harps, assisted with the organisation of Cuchulain's.

Cuchulain's coaches found inspiring a team in Pollock extremely difficult in an exceptionally poor and deprived area of the city where discipline and organisation meant little to many of the children involved with the club. When the players of the Pollock team accessed some hurling sticks they attacked the visiting members of another team and were sardonically labelled Glasgow's first modern hurling team.

Although training and coaching began and several matches were played little became of Cuchulain's. Much of the club's organisation was handicapped when Doherty decided to return to his roots in Donegal. John Nally subsequently moved the team to a more receptive eastern Glasgow base and renamed the new club, Michael Davitt's.

Derryvale, Glasgow (1993–1995)

Previously involved with Pearse Harps, Tommy Millar began to organise a youth set under the banner of Derryvale, the club name recognising his own roots in County Derry. Although operating during a high point in the success of youth football the club was also inhibited by drawing its players from the same area in Glasgow as Tir Conail Harps and Mulroy Gaels.

However, Derryvale made one notable impact on the game in successfully attracting players from the local Asian community while also making its mark in nearby non-denominational schools, thus drawing players from outwith the typical Irish community in the south side of Glasgow.

Dundee Dalriada (1989–)

Initial efforts to begin a gaelic football team in Dundee were instigated by Peter Mossey from Gortin, County Tyrone, whilst a student at the City's university in the late 1970s and early 1980s. Though failing at this period, it was another set of students from Ireland who resurrected the idea and began a club in late 1989. Declan Curran from Tyrone, Barry Grimes and Ian Hannon from Armagh canvassed around the university as well as in the Lochee district of the city, an area known locally as 'little Tipperary', due to a high percentage of its inhabitants originating from Ireland, especially in the late 19th century.

With some assistance from the university sports council an area of ground at Riverside was secured for training and playing. Almost all of the players of the developing club were Irish born students, with the exception of two former Sands MacSwiney players who had moved to Dundee to work, Paul Lennon and James 'Jinky' Gilmour. 1993 All-Ireland final squad member with Derry, Stephen Mulvenna (formally Antrim), also played for the team during its formative period. The first match played by the club was a successful challenge match against Beltane Shamrocks in Wishaw.

In January 1990 a meeting was held amongst the players of the new club at St Francis Friary, Dundee. In February, the club, headed by president, Father Eugene O Sullivan from Kilkenny, also a founder in 1973 of Tayforth Shinty Club, affiliated to the Glasgow County Board. Until this point in time the club had been known as Dundee Fianna. However, with the latter part of the name meaning soldiers/warriors, some players believed that this could prove contentious due to its possible political connotations by those hostile to things Irish. By a narrow vote the name was changed to the less contentious and Celtic connotive, Dundee Dalriada: Dalriada being the name of the gaelic tribe who had came to the south west Argyllshire coast of Scotland from Ireland during the 6th century, and, who later contributed to the founding of the Kingdom of Scotland.

Since playing its first competitive match in early 1990, periodically Dundee proved one of the best sides in Scotland during the most recent resurgence. However, with a club consisting almost entirely of Irish born university based players this also gave those who live in the area numerous problems in sustaining an adequate side throughout the season.

Subsequent to being beaten in the final at Pearse Park by Sands MacSwiney's in 1991, Dundee won the County Championship in 1992 and 1993. In 1993, after defeating Birmingham's John Mitchells' and Southern Gaels of Poole, Dundee reached the final of the British Provincial Club Championship, losing 0:15 to 1:10 to one of the best clubs in England during the same period, Tirconail Gaels of London. For its efforts in becoming the first club from Scotland to win two Provincial matches in recent decades, Dundee were recipients of an Irish Post club award in 1993. Remarkably, the Dalriada panel of that year contained several players from the village of Glin, County Limerick, all students attending University in Dundee.

Dunedin Connolly's, Edinburgh (1988–)

Edinburgh has contained a large immigrant Irish population since the middle of the 19th century. In the late 1980s this was reflected in the emergence of a gaelic football club. The club took its description from the gaelic name for the city and from one of the leaders of the 1916 Easter Uprising in Ireland, Edinburgh born of immigrant parents, James Connolly.

During his photographic travels covering Irish events in Scotland, the Irish Post's correspondent in Scotland, Tommy Main, found himself an important link between a number of groups and individuals. Developing an interest in Irish cultural activities, Main was also to promote some of these activities by way of encouragement and publicity. Thus emerged Dunedin Connolly's. After much prompting, Tony Haughey from Belfast and Benny McGinley began to think seriously about starting a club to compete in the growing gaelic scene in the west. In 1988, at a regular Irish function held at the St Mary's Star of the Sea Catholic Parish in the Leith area of the city, also attended by Father Sweeney of Beltane Shamrock's and Clan na Gael Gaelic Clubs', some of these individuals came together to form the Edinburgh team. Among them was a strong Donegal and Mayo representation. In 1989 the club played its first competitive match.

Most of the original players of the Connolly's club lived in the Liberton/Gilmerton area of the city. However, by 1991/92 the club succeeded in attracting a number of Irish born players who lived in the city or who attended Edinburgh or Heriot-Watt Universities. With a growing Irish born base, and therefore a more experienced network of gaelic footballers, in 1991 the club began to emerge from its youthful beginnings. In that season it reached the semi-final of the Championship and rested at fourth in the league competition. Players such as Neal O Doherty from Kildare, Oliver McKenna, Ciaran McLarnon and Mick Mulvihill all began to make their mark within the game in Scotland. During the same season the club also secured use of a home park in the grounds of St Augustine's School in the Broomhouse area.

In a final played at the home of Beltane Shamrock's in Wishaw in 1992, Connolly's won its first trophy, the O Fiaich Cup, defeating rivals Mulroy Gaels 0:11 to 1:7. During 1993 the club continued to gain a strong current of players through links with Heriot-Watt University. A number of former players with the Heriot-Watt based gaelic football team decided to live and work in the area and the local side reaped the benefits. In 1994 an influx of players made a marked difference to both the depth and quality of the Edinburgh squad. Connolly's reached the final of the 1994 Championship and after drawing the first match against Dundee, the Edinburgh side easily won the replay at Pearse Park by 3:10 to 0:5. Connolly's also won both the County seven-a side tournament and the Pearse Cup in 1996.

By 1996 the club contained none of the players or members who had instigated Dunedin Connolly's. By then the club had attracted manager Frank Gallagher from St Brendan's of London, under his management previously winners of the prestigious London County Championship. Gallagher hailed originally from Ballyshannon in County Donegal. In the same year, positive relations with Duddingston based Edinburgh rugby team, Portobello FP, led to the decision to move to that club's large playing area where a pitch was set aside for gaelic football.

Glencovitt Rovers, Clydebank (1991–)

Former St Patrick's player and assistant, Jimmy Kelly, returned to live in the eastern Glasgow conurbation of Clydebank in the early 1990s. Kelly's roots lay in County Antrim and his return to Clydebank was the catalyst for the re-emergence of gaelic football in the area in March 1991. Donegal born players, Danny Friel and Colm Doherty, were important as the new club began to recruit and participate in competitions. Locals like Mark Docherty, Stuart McDonald and Mick Timoney were introduced to the game by Kelly and until 1997 remained important players for the club.

Although there had been a G.A.A. club, Roger Casements, in the area a number of decades previously, the current club's name was chosen when Colm Doherty on visiting his home in Donegal, returned with a couple of footballs courtesy of a former schoolmaster. The school was located in Glencovitt, Ballybofey, and that was the name adopted by the new Clydebank team.

After briefly using facilities in the shape of a converted rugby pitch in Dumbarton the council in Clydebank eventually provided local playing facilities at Strauss Avenue. Although facilities were poor and the pitch was extremely small, the club was finally locally based. Glencovitt raised its profile with the visits of, as well as visits to Dublin based G.A.A. club, Good Council of Drimnagh.

The Dublin club was subsequently requested to play in a combined rules Hurling/Shinty match to celebrate the centenary of the West Highland Railway Line in Scotland in 1994. Assisted by John Gallagher, during the period 1993–94, Kelly attempted to introduce youth football to the area. Although this was a short venture due to a lack of support, several of the young people involved retained a degree of interest in the sport.

In 1996, amidst local Government restructuring, Glencovitt lost its playing facilities. In terms of the games promotion, having no home venue or training facilities proved a major problem for the club. For Kelly, the resultant travel costs and lack of local sponsorship and focal point took a heavy toll on the progress of gaelic activities in the area. Nonetheless, Glencovitt did manage to win its first trophy in season 1996. The 'B' Championship was won using Doherty, Docherty, McDonald and Timoney, as well as others such as Richard Gough (Australia), Ciaran McCrory (Tyrone) and Paddy Keenan (Louth).

Michael Davitt's, Glasgow (1993–1996)

Inspired by John Nally, who had previously gained playing and organisational experience with Pearse Harps and Cuchulain's, and assisted by Charlie McCluskey and Tim Porter, Davitt's emerged in the wake of the demise of Cuchulain's in Pollock. As Cuchulain's demised their existing resources were transferred to Davitt's.

164

Davitt's was an under age club which participated in primary school competition as well as under 12 football. The club drew substantially from St Anne's Primary School located near Celtic Park, trained at Glasgow Green and played fixtures at a number of venues in the city. The club were noted for the first modern appointment of an Irish language officer in John Lee from Dublin, also sponsor of the team and owner of local Irish bar, The Squirrel.

Mulroy Gaels, Glasgow (1984–)

Mulroy were re-started in 1984/85 by Seamus Sweeney, a Glasgow based contractor who originated from Fanad in County Donegal. The first side was made up of players mainly from Rathmullen and Fanad in Donegal as well as a number of Scottish born players whose roots lay in the same area of north west Ireland. Players, Neil Boyle, Liam Sheridan, John Crowe and Mick Shiels remained with Mulroy for most of the period of Glasgow's gaelic football resurgence.

Former player, Eddie Canning (Donegal) was a significant contributor to Mulroy's youth policy during the first half of the 1990s, although this initiative faded due to a lack of assistance on the part of other adult members of the club. Nonetheless, during this time the club enjoyed success at minor level.

Although having failed in a number of Championships finals and semi-finals, Mulroy have proved to be the most successful club in recent G.A.A. history in Scotland. The club has won every trophy available including the Championship in 1989, 1995 and 1997, as well as recording a remarkable run of successive league titles between 1985 and 1994. In 1989, Mulroy lost narrowly to St Vincent's of Luton in the British Provincial Championship.

Pearse Harps, Glasgow (1985–1993)

As a result of the efforts of Father Eamonn Sweeney and Mick Moran, Pearse Harps were constituted as a club during 1984–85. The club began competing during the season of revival in 1985. Based at Pearse Park in Cambuslang, Pearse drew its players from various parts of Glasgow as well as having a strong representation from Coatbridge.

Continuing links with games in the 1960s and 1970s, this came via the efforts of Pat O Callaghan from Armagh, who played football in the area for three decades. O Callaghan also played beside his son who became one of the most able of the young breed of second generation Irish playing gaelic sports. Others players such as Eddie McHugh from Tyrone likewise played in earlier decades. Pearse became a club which offered solid competition for the other teams. Its greatest moment arriving in season 1986 when the club won the Pearse Cup (formally Summer Cup) against Mulroy Gaels at Pearse Park, a ground shared by both sides.

During September of 1986 Pearse Harps visited Letterkenny in Donegal, Maghera County Derry, Crossmaglen in County Armagh and Ardoyne in Belfast to play local sides. On returning to Scotland, the Coatbridge based players departed to set up a club in their own area. Around the same time, a group of young men were motivated to begin football training in the Garngad district of the city. The hope was that they might join with Pearse Harps to form a strong city based club. A number of these players were drawn towards gaelic football because of its perceived political connotations. However, after a handful of training sessions only one or two pursued any further contact with gaelic sports.

Although the departure of Coatbridge players initially had an effect on the numbers involved with Pearse, it maintained its status and enjoyed a presence for a number of years. During the early 1990s the Club, influenced by Tommy Main, John Nally, Mick Hollinger and Mick Moran, began a number of minor teams. These sides proved to be both successful and attractive in relation to numbers and the games promotion. However, the ambitions of the minor section were not matched by those of the seniors and eventually Pearse's minor administrators began to look for other avenues to pursue its potential. This culminated in the evolution of Tir Conail Harps. However, this also had a detrimental effect upon Pearse and by 1993 Pearse Harps found it increasingly difficult to field full strength sides and this led to the club's demise during the season.

Saint Malachy's, Chapelhall and Calderbank (1992–1993)

St Malachy's were inspired by Armaghman Sean Duffy who was a player in Glasgow during the 1960s and 1970s as well as being Secretary of the County Board of Scotland in the early 1990s. Involving mainly primary school children from the local Corpus Christi and St Aloysius schools in his adopted Chapelhall and

Calderbank areas of Lanarkshire, St Malachy's played several challenge and competitive matches. However, the club demised when Duffy departed the County Board in late 1993.

Saint Patrick's, Dumbarton (1984–)

As was the pattern in Glasgow G.A.A. matters, the first games held in 1984 were of a mixed team nature and these games often involved players from Dumbarton. In Dumbarton, schoolteacher Eamonn Cullen started the St Patrick's Gaelic Football Club, taking its name from the town's Catholic school which was to provide the main base for the club's future. Along with fellow St Pat's teachers Donald Hoey, Jimmy Grimes and Gerry Carey, as well as Jimmy Kelly, future founder of the Glencovitt Club in Clydebank, and relying initially on friends from the local Leven Rugby Club, St Patrick's began to field a regular side. The first squad of players to represent the town in gaelic football consisted of:

Steven Mairs, Michael Docherty, Paul Ferguson, Jimmy Grimes, Andy Young, Donald Hoey, Gary Casey, Saul Docherty, Sean McDonald, Gerry Carey, Martin Hannan, Eamonn Cullen, Paul McGrogan, Bobby Neil and Robert Floyd.

By the time the club won the Scotland County championship in 1996, beating Sands MacSwiney's in the final played at Coatbridge, Cullen remained manager, Mairs was the goalkeeper and Docherty had by then regularly captained the club for ten years. This was also the first occasion when a club in Britain had won a championship final with a team totally comprising local born players.

St Patrick's role of honour has been impressive. Championship winners three times, league winners once and runners up seven times; four times O Fiaich Cup (previously the Autumn Cup) winners, and British Provincial Championship semi-finalists in 1987 and 1996. In 1988 and 1993, Dumbarton District Council elected St Patrick's as its team of the year. St Patrick's players have also represented the Glasgow and Scotland County Boards on numerous occasions. This is particularly so in the case in minor football, an area where the club has pursued an active policy. The club also has the best council owned G.A.A. facilities in Scotland, at Posties Park, Dumbarton.

The roots of the club is reflected in the regular visits to Ireland to play gaelic football. Donegal, Dublin, Kildare, Louth, Meath,

Galway and Mayo have all formed part of the St Patrick's itinerary over the years. St Patrick's have also hosted clubs from Kildare, Louth, Dublin, Donegal, Leeds, Huddersfield, Leicester and Luton.

Sands MacSwiney's, Coatbridge (1986–)

Founded by Joe Bradley whose roots lie in the Irish midlands and west Ulster, and assisted by Joe Reilly whose people immigrated to Glenboig in Lanarkshire from County Westmeath and Baltinglass, County Wicklow, Sands developed from Pearse Harps in Glasgow. As the numbers of Coatbridge players began to increase with the Glasgow based club some Coatbridge members believed it would be more appropriate to give birth to a local based team in an area previously renowned for its gaelic sports activities.

Sands first full season was marked by success in reaching the 1986 final of the Glasgow Championship only to lose to St Patrick's. By 1988 Sands won their first major trophy winning the O Fiaich Cup beating Beltane Shamrock's in the final held at Pearse Park. The same cup was won by Sands in season 1996 beating St Patrick's in the final held at Dumbarton. The Coatbridge team won the Championship in 1990 and 1991, were runners up in 1986, 1989 and 1996, and also won the Pearse Cup in 1990. Sands have been regular contributors to the County team and initiated its own minor set up in the early 1990s. The club also initiated a successful local schools tournament during 1996 and 1997 and this involved approximately one hundred and fifty boys and girls from local primary schools.

Sands MacSwiney's have been frequent visitors to Ireland over the years and have made the Glasgow September holiday weekend the club's time for returning to its roots. Since jointly visiting Maghera County Derry, Crossmaglen County Armagh, Letterkenny County Donegal and Belfast County Antrim with Pearse Harps in 1986, Sands have visited clubs in Gortin, County Tyrone, Killarney, County Kerry, Nobber, County Meath, Ballybay, County Monaghan, Ardoyne and Falls Road, Belfast, and have been frequent visitors to Watty Grahams Glen, Maghera, County Derry. The club has also hosted a number of teams from Mayo, Derry, Monaghan, Leeds as well as the County Sligo senior squad as part of the County Board of Scotland's centenary celebrations in 1997. In 1994, Micky Moran, coach of 1993 All-Ireland football winners Derry, brought the Sam Maguire trophy to Coatbridge to display to local football enthusiasts.

Shotts Gaels (1996–)

The village of Shotts in west Lanarkshire was introduced to gaelic sports during the period 1994/95. Martin McCulloch and Thomas Larkin, formally footballers with Beltane Shamrock's, inaugurated children's football, camogie and finally a senior football club which made its debut in April 1997.

Supported by a few local businessmen as well as North Lanarkshire Council, Shotts Gaels were able to make headway due in the main to the aid of the local Catholic parish priest and council at Saint Patrick's Church. During the Summer of 1996, several club members attended a Summer camp organised by St Peter's G.A.A Club of Dunboyne, County Meath. Around the same time the Club was guest of the Dublin County Board, while it also hosted a camogie/shinty tournament involving the local club, Tir Conail Harps, Oban Shinty Club as well as Lochgilphead Shinty Club.

Tir Conail Harps, Glasgow (1994–)

Tir Conail is one of the youngest clubs' on the Scottish gaelic scene. Formed in 1994, other gaels admire the efforts, organisation and resources of this strongly linked Donegal based club. The involvement of Tommy Main with the gaelic scene in the mid to late 1980s proved a boon to the G.A.A. Increasingly drawn towards Pearse Harps in Glasgow, and recognising that youth would provide the future of gaelic sports in the west of Scotland, Main began to recruit young members to form a number of youth sides in the Pearse Harps set-up. However, with a lack of organisation and little to show for their efforts with Pearse, Main, along with some interested individuals, decided to form their own club.

Drawing mainly on the south side of Glasgow, recruitment by the Tir Conail Club invariably tapped an area rich in recent Donegal immigration, thus the name of the new club. Beginning with a variety of under-age teams, by 1997 Tir Conail contained under 10, 12, 14 and 16 squads as well a young side who entered the senior grade for the first time: overall around twelve teams. By 1997 the club operated with membership numbers of between 150 and 200. This also included a camogie side which played regular matches against Lochgilphead Ladies Shinty Club in the north west of Scotland, as well as an aspiring ladies gaelic football team. In November 1997, Tir Conail won its first trophy, the B League in a final against Paisley Gaels.

Few gaelic clubs travel to other counties to compete in gaelic competitions in a similar fashion to Tir Conail. In 1995 its dominant youth side travelled to England to win the under 12 British Provincial Championship. The Glasgow club set a British Provincial record in the same year having teams in three provincial finals. As a result, the club was awarded a prestigious *Irish Post* Club of the Year Award in 1997.

The club has also competed in matches all over Britain and Ireland. In Britain the club won the St Brendan's seven a side tournament in Manchester in 1996. Visits to Ireland have included Ballycroy, County Mayo, Ballycastle, County Antrim and Falcarragh, County Donegal. At McHale Park, Castlebar in 1996, the Glasgow players were defeated by Dicksboro of Kilkenny in the final of the prestigious annual Peil na nOg competition in Ireland. Tir Conail has also hosted a number of clubs from both Ireland and Britain.

Much of the success of the Tir Conail club is due to the efforts of some of their members to draw on as wide a local population as possible. As a result, in the mid 1990s several schools in the south side of Glasgow have become accustomed to members coaching their pupils, among them; St Fillan's, St Jude's, St Bridget's, St Bride's and Holy Cross primary schools.

APPENDIX 3

THE GAELIC ATHLETIC ASSOCIATION IN THE REST OF BRITAIN

The G.A.A. in England has also recognised that its games cannot exist without the involvement of second and third generation Irish. In presenting the London County Board (the largest individual unit outside of Ireland) with a special award to mark its centenary of 1996, the *Irish Post* believed:

> The formation of the London Minor Board has proved to be a remarkable success, and has ensured that the board can look ahead to another 100 years of promoting our native games.

London has played a significant role in G.A.A. history and Michael Collins, Liam MacCarthy and Sam Maguire, figures involved in the struggle for Irish independence in the early part of the 20th century, all played gaelic sports in London.

Chairman of the London County Board, John Lacey, viewed the holding of the G.A.A.'s 1996 convention in centenary celebrating London as 'a manifestation of the policy to embrace all Gaels and an effort to enable all exiles to be part of the movement initiated in Thurles in 1884'. By the time of the convention in 1996, London contained twelve hurling and forty-five football clubs. The London championship winning teams also participate in the national league competitions held in Ireland every year from October to April.

Not only in London but in other parts of England have gaelic games developed. Previously organised as a division of the London County, in 1960 the Herefordshire County Board was formed by a small group under the leadership of its first founder chairman, Father Jerome O Hanlon, a native of Lombard, County Cork. The first board had nine clubs in affiliation. In 1995 Herefordshire's junior hurlers won their first All-Ireland title beating Tyrone in the final played at Luton.

Gloucestershire formed its first gaelic hurling club The Emmetts, in 1928. Although it was the early 1950s before it began to make a mark, the first county board was founded in the area in 1949.

Experiencing many years of struggle to survive, like a number of other counties, Gloucestershire turned its attentions towards youth development as the number of young Irish immigrants arriving in Britain began to fall.

St Annes of Keighly, who had previously played its matches in Lancashire due to a lack of local competition, was one of the original gaelic clubs in Yorkshire which in 1949 formed the first County Board spearheaded by Father Donal Stritch. In the same year famous Yorkshire gaelic clubs' like Hugh O Neills and St Brendans of Leeds were also founded. Struggling to survive as Irish immigration to Yorkshire began to diminish, if not halt, in 1977 the County gave birth to a minor board which proved to be the key to endurance. Although by the mid 1990s having only six clubs, the G.A.A. in Yorkshire remains a focus for Irish identity.

In the English midlands in the 1990s gaelic sports have also been vibrant. Ex-patriot communities throughout Birmingham, Coventry, Wolverhampton, Leicester, Derby, Nottingham, Northampton and Corby have traditionally supported clubs of both a football and hurling affiliation. The 1920s saw the birth of gaelic games in this county whilst the oldest surviving club has been John Mitchell's of Birmingham, founded in 1940. The Warwickshire County Board was formed in 1944. By 1995 Warwickshire contained twenty-seven hurling and football clubs as well camogie and football sections amongst women.

In Lancashire the first club was founded in 1895 under the auspices of the Liverpool County Board which subsequently became the Lancashire County Board. Activity to promote under age gaelic games during the 1970s in Lancashire meant that by the mid 1990s, the county sustained six clubs.

Although many clubs in Britain struggle to operate either successfully or even to exist, many others are centres of vibrancy and are significant focus for Irish identity. In the 1990s, the G.A.A. in Britain remains the largest Irish community organisation in the country.

APPENDIX 4

DIRECTORY: GAELIC ATHLETIC ASSOCIATION COISTE ALBAIN

Coatbridge Gaels
c/o Pat McHugh
28 Mauldslie Street
Coatbridge
Lanarkshire
ML5 4AA

Tel. 01236 431898

Dundee Dalriada
c/o Peter Mossey
The Auld Smiddy
Perthshire
PH2 7SU

Tel. 01821 670332

Dunedin Connolly's
c/o Frank Gallaghlloch
24 Milton Crescent
Edinburgh
EH15 3PQ

Tel. 0131 669 5383

Glencovitt Rovers
c/o Jim Kelly
17 Cambridge Avenue
Clydebank
G81 2JB

Tel. 0141 562 7182

Mulroy Gaels
c/o Ann Maria Millar
22 Hollybrook Street
Govanhill, Glasgow
G42 7EH

Tel. 0141 569 8416

St Patrick's
c/o Eamon Cullen
66 Cardross Road
Dumbarton
G82 4JQ

Tel. 01389 761010

Sands MacSwiney's
c/o Sean McGleenan
Osprey Dr
Uddingston
Lanarkshire
G71 6HR

Tel. 01698 817099

Shotts Gaels
c/o Martin McCulloch
3 Glen Road
Shotts
ML7 5EA

Tel. 01501 825498

Tir Conail Harps
c/o Tommy Main
6 Daisy Street
Glasgow
G42 8AY

Tel. 0141 423 7824

Paisley Gaels
c/o Michael Hollinger
32 Aurs Crescent
Barrhead
G78 ZL4

Tel. 0141 580 5609

Other G.A.A. contacts in Scotland

Roisin Campbell (County Board Treasurer 1997/98)
  (Glasgow) 0141 571 4906

Maire Hughes (County Board Secretary 1997/98)
  (Glasgow) 0141 883 8435

Charlie McCluskey (County Board)
  (Glasgow) 0141 554 5208

John Nally (County Board)
  (Glasgow) 0141 556 2198

Billy Nugent (Solicitor to the GAA in Scotland)
  (Glasgow) 0141 554 1016

Fr Eamon Sweeney (Coatbridge) 01236 606808

Apart from Dunedin Connolly's in the east, Dundee Dalriada in the north east and Shotts Gaels in the central belt, all clubs in Scotland are located in the west. St Patrick's and Glencovitt are situated to the west of Glasgow as is Paisley Gaels. Mulroy Gaels and Tir Lonail Harps serve the south side of Glasgow while Coatbridge Gaels and Sands MacSwiney's draw players from Lanarkshire and the eastern half of the Glasgow area.

APPENDIX 5
GAELIC ATHLETIC CLUBS IN SCOTLAND
1897–1997

Ayrshire Gaels (Saltcoats)
Beltane Shamrocks (Wishaw)
Brian Boru (Blantyre)
Cavan Slashers (Glasgow)
Clan na hEireann (Glasgow)
Clan na Gael (Hamilton)
Clan na Gael (Glasgow)
Clan na Ghaeldhilge (Springburn, Glasgow)
Coatbridge (Hurling club)
Coatbridge Gaels (Coatbridge)
Cuchulains (Polmadie, Glasgow)
Cuchulains (Dumbarton)
Cuchulains (Glasgow)
Dalcassians (Carfin)
Derryvale (Glasgow)
Desmonds (Wishaw)
Dr Crokes (Dumbarton)
Dundee Dalriada (Dundee)
Dunedin Connollys (Edinburgh)
Eire Og (Gorbals, Glasgow)
Eire Og (Port Glasgow))
Eire Og (Coatbridge)
Emmets (Hamilton)
Eugene O Growneys (Glasgow)
Fag an Bealach (Sons of Erin, Carfin)
Falkirk (gaelic football and hurling club)
Faughs Hurling Club (Glasgow)
Fianna Fireann (Glasgow)
Finn MacCumhails (Anderston and Partick, Glasgow)
Fintan Lalors (Govan, Glasgow)
Fitzgeralds (Glasgow)
Glasgow Camogie Club
Glencovitt Rovers (Clydebank))
Granuailes (Glasgow)
Hibernians (Pollockshaws, Glasgow)
Lambh Dearg (Cleland)
Lambh Dearg (Kinning Park, Glasgow)

Lord Edwards (Motherwell)
McCurtain Gaels (Springburn, Glasgow)
Mulroy Gaels (Glasgow)
O Tooles (Kinning Park, Glasgow)
Owen Roe O Neill (Coatbridge)
Paisley Gaels (1940s and 1950s)
Paisley Gaels (Paisley, 1990s–)
Patrick Sarsfields (Coatbridge)
Padraic Pearses (south-east Glasgow)
Pearse Harps (Glasgow, 1920s)
Pearse Harps (Glasgow, 1980s–)
Rapparees (Glasgow)
Red Hugh O Neills (Glasgow)
Roger Casements (Paisley)
Rosses Rovers (Glasgow)
Round Towers (Scotstown, Glasgow)
Rovers (Cambuslang, Glasgow)
Sands MacSwineys (Coatbridge)
Sarsfields (Greenock)
Shotts Gaels (Shotts, Lanarkshire)
South O Hanlons (Glasgow)
St Brendans (Glasgow)
St Colmcilles (Edinburgh)
St Eunans (Clydebank)
St Francis (Falkirk)
St Malachys (Chapelhall & Calderbank)
St Margarets (Airdrie)
St Marks (Carntyne, Glasgow)
St Patricks (Dumbarton)
St Patricks (Greenock)
St Patricks (Wishaw)
Taras (Gourock)
Tara Harps (Bridgeton, Glasgow)
Thomas Davis (Motherwell)
Tir Conail Harps (Glasgow)
Wishaw Shamrocks (Wishaw)

BIBLIOGRAPHY

Adams G: *The Politics of Irish Freedom*, Brandon Books, Kerry, 1986.

Allison L: *The Politics of Sport*, Manchester University Press, 1986.

Beresford D: *Ten Men Dead*, Grafton Books, London, 1987.

Boyle R and Haynes R: 'The Grand old game': football, media and identity in Scotland, in, *Media, Culture and Society*, vol 18, no 4, pp. 549–564, 1996.

Bradley J M: *Ethnic and Religious Identity in Modern Scotland*: Avebury, 1995 (A).

Bradley J M: Intermarriage, Education, and Discrimination, in T M Devine, edt, *St Mary's Hamilton: A Social History 1846–1996*, John Donald, Edinburgh, pp. 83–94, 1995. (B)

Bradley J M: Profile of a Roman Catholic Parish in Scotland, in *Scottish Affairs*, No 14, Winter, pp. 123–139, 1996.

Bradley J M: Identity, Politics and Culture: Orangeism in Scotland, in *Scottish Affairs*, No 16, Summer, pp. 104–128, 1996.

Bradley J M: Facets of the Irish Diaspora: 'Irishness' in 20th Century Scotland, in, *Irish Journal of Sociology*, vol 6, 1996. (C)

Brown S J: Outside the Covenant: The Scottish Presbyterian Churches and Irish Immigration, 1922–1938, in *The Innes Review*, Volume XL11, No 1, Spring, pp. 19–45, 1991.

Campbell T and Woods P: *The Glory and The Dream, The History of Celtic FC, 1887–1986*: Mainstream Publishing, 1986.

Canning Rev B J: *Padraig H Pearse and Scotland*. Published by Padraig Pearse Centenary Commemoration Committee, Glasgow, 1979.

Cassidy L: Faded Pictures from Irish Town, in *Causeway*, pp. 34–38, Autumn, 1996.

Celt: Sporting Nationalism: A look at the political origins of the G.A.A., *IRIS*, no 4, Nov, pp. 25–26, 1982.

Celt: Changing the Rules: A look at the political origins of the G.A.A., *IRIS*, no 5, March, pp. 30–31, 1983.

Coakley J J: *Sport in Society: Issues and Controversies*, Mosby, Colerado, 1990.

Cooney J: *Scotland and the Papacy*, Paul Harris, Edinburgh, 1982.

Cronin M: Defenders of the Nation? The Gaelic Athletic Association and Irish Nationalist Identity, in *Irish Political Studies*, 11, pp. 1–19, 1996.

Curtice J and Gallagher: in Jowell R, Witherspoon S, Brook L, edts: *British Social Attitudes; the 7th report*: Social and Community Planning Research, Gower Publishing, pp. 183–216, 1990.

Curtis L: Ireland *The Propaganda War*: Pluto Press, 1984.

Curtis L: *Nothing But The Same Old Story: The roots of Anti-Irish Racism*: Published by Information on Ireland, 5th edition, 1988.

Davis G: *The Irish In Britain 1815–1914*: Gill and Macmillan, 1991.

De Burca: *The G.A.A: A History of the Gaelic Athletic Association*, Cumann Luthchleas Gael, Dublin, 1980.

De Burca M: *The Story of the G.A.A*, Wolfhound Press, Dublin, 1990.

Devine T M, (edt): *Irish Immigrants and Scottish Society in the Nineteenth and Twentieth Centuries; Proceedings of the Scottish Historical Studies Seminar*: University of Strathclyde, 1989/90, John Donald Publishers Ltd, 1991.

Devine T M (edt): *St Mary's Hamilton: A Social History, 1846–1996*, John Donald, Edinburgh, 1995.

Feehan J M: *Bobby Sands and the Tragedy of Northern Ireland*, Mercier Press, Dublin and Cork, 1984.

Finley R J: Nationalism, Race, Religion And The Irish Question In Inter-War Scotland, in, *The Innes Review*, Vol. XLII, No 1, Spring, pp. 46–67, 1991.

Finn G P T: Racism, Religion and Social Prejudice: Irish Catholic Clubs, Soccer and Scottish Society — 1 The Historical Roots of Prejudice in *The International Journal of the History of Sport*, 8, 1, pp. 72–95, 1991.

Finn G P T: Racism, Religion and Social Prejudice: Irish Catholic Clubs, Soccer and Scottish Society — 11 Social Identities and Conspiracy Theories, in *The International Journal of the History of Sport*, 8, 3, pp. 370–397, 1991.

Finn G P T: Faith, Hope and Bigotry: Case Studies of Anti-Catholic Prejudice in Scottish Soccer and Society; in *Scottish*

Sport in the Making of the Nation: Ninety-Minute Patriots, Leicester University Press, 1994.

Finn G P T: Sporting Symbols, Sporting Identities: Soccer and Intergroup Conflict in Scotland and Northern Ireland, pp. 33–55, in, *Scotland and Ulster*, Edt by I S Wood, Mercat Press, Edinburgh, 1994.

Finn G P T: Series of papers lodged with Jordanhill Library, Strathclyde University on the role of conspiracy in anti-Catholicism in Scotland and Northern Ireland, 1990–1994.

Flanagan C: *Sport in a Divided Society: the Role of the G.A.A. in Northern Ireland*, Unpublished post-graduate thesis, Faculty of Humanities, University of Ulster, 1991.

Gallagher C: *The Gaelic Athletic Association in London*. Research project held by the Irish Studies Centre, University of North London, 1993.

Gallagher T: *Glasgow The Uneasy Peace*: Manchester University Press, 1987.

Gallagher T: *The Catholic Irish in Scotland: In Search of Identity* in T M Devine (edt) Irish Immigrants and Scottish Society in the Nineteenth and Twentieth Centuries; John Donald Publishers Limited, Edinburgh, 1991.

Gilley S & Swift R, edts: *The Irish in the Victorian City*: Croom Helm, London, 1985.

Handley J E: *The Irish in Scotland*: John S Burns & Sons, Glasgow. (this book incorporates both The Irish in Scotland 1798–1845 and The Irish in Modern Scotland. 1943 & 1947. Cork University Press), 1964.

Handley J E: *The Celtic Story*: Stanley Paul, London, 1960.

Hargreaves J, (edt): *Sport, Culture and Ideology*, Routledge, pp. 30–61, 1982.

Hayes M: Myths and Matches, in *Causeway, cultural traditions journal*, Summer, 1997.

Healy P: *Irish Nationalism and the Origins of the Gaelic Athletic Association*. Unpublished Dissertation, History B.A. degree, University of North London, 1994.

Hickman M: *A study of the incorporation of the Irish in Britain with special reference to Catholic state education: involving a comparison of the attitudes of pupils and teachers in selected Catholic schools in London and Liverpool*, unpublished PhD, University of London, 1990.

Hickman M: *Religion, Class and Identity. The State, the Catholic Church and the Education of the Irish in Britain*, Avebury, Aldershot, 1995.

Hoberman J: *Sport and Political Ideology*, Heinemann, London, 1984.

Holmes M: Symbols of National Identity: The Case of the Irish National Football Team, in *Irish Political Studies*, 9, pp. 81–98, 1994.

Holt R: Sport and History: The State of the Subject in Britain, in *Twentieth Century British History*, vol 7, No 2, pp. 231–252, 1996.

Humphries T: *Green Fields: Gaelic Sport In Ireland*, Weidenfield and Nicolson, London, 1996.

Hutchinson R: *Camanachd: The Story of Shinty*, Mainstream Publishing, Edinburgh, 1989.

Inglis J: The Irish In Britain: A Question Of Identity, in *Irish Studies in Britain* No 3, Spring/Summer 1982.

Isajiw W. W: Definitions of Ethnicity, in, *Ethnicity*, vol 1, no 2, July, pp 111–124, 1974.

Jarvie G, Walker G (edts): *Scottish Sport in the Making of the Nation; Ninety Minute Patriots*, Leicester University Press, 1994.

Jenkins R: *The thistle and the grail*, MacDonald and Co, Glasgow, 1983.

Kee R: *The Most Distressful Country*, volume one of the Green Flag, Quartet Books, London, 1976.

Kendrick S: Scotland, Social Change and Politics, in, *The Making of Scotland: Nation, Culture and Social Change*, D McCrone, D Kendrick and P Straw (edts), Edinburgh University Press, 1989.

Kircaldy J: Irish Jokes: No Cause For Laughter, *Irish Studies in Britain*, No 2, Autumn/Winter 1981.

Kinealy C: *This Great Calamity: The Irish Famine 1845–52*, Gill and Macmillan Ltd, 1994.

Longley E: Paths to the academy, *Fortnight*, p. 26, December 1996.

Mandle W F: The Irish Republican Brotherhood and the beginnings of the Gaelic Athletic Association, *Irish Historical Studies*, xx, 80, pp. 418–38, 1977.

Mandle W F: *The G.A.A. and Irish Nationalist Politics*, Helm, Gill and MacMillan, Dublin, 1987.

Mitchell J: Religion And Politics In Scotland, Unpublished paper presented to *Seminar on Religion and Scottish Politics*, University of Edinburgh 1992.

Muirhead, Rev. I. A: Catholic Emancipation: Scottish Reactions in 1829 *Innes Review,* 24, 1, Spring, 1973.

Muirhead, Rev. I. A: 'Catholic Emancipation in Scotland: the debate and the aftermath,' *Innes Review*, 24, 2, Autumn, 1973.

Mullan M: Opposition, Social Closure, and Sport: The Gaelic Athletic Association in the 19th Century, *Sociology of Sport Journal*, 12, pp. 268–289, 1995.

MacLennan H D: *Shinty: 100 Years of the Camanachd Association*, Balnain Books, Nairn, 1993.

MacLua, B: *The Steadfast Rule: a history of the G.A.A. ban*, Press Cuchulainn Ltd, Dublin, 1967.

McFarland E W: *Protestants First: Orangeism in 19th Century Scotland*, Edinburgh University Press, 1990.

O Ceallaigh S: *Story of the G.A.A.*, Published by Gaelic Athletic Publications, Limerick, 1977.

O'Conner K: *The Irish in Britain*, Torc, Dublin, 1970.

O Farrell P: *Ireland's English Question*, New York, 1972.

O Hehir M: *The G.A.A. 100 Years*, Gill and MacMillan, Dublin, 1984.

O Malley E: *On Another Man's Wound*, Anvil Books Ltd, Dublin, 1979

O Tuathaigh M A G: The Irish in Nineteenth Century Britain: Problems of Integration, pp. 13–36, in Gilley and Swift, *The Irish in the Victorian City*, 1985.

Phoenix E: 'G.A.A.'s Era of Turmoil in Northern Ireland', *Fortnight*, pp. 8–9, 17 December 1984.

Puirseal P: *The G.A.A. in its time*, Published by the Purcell Family, Carrigeen, Dublin, 1982.

Quinn J: *Ulster Football and Hurling: The Path of Champions*, Wolfhound Press, Dublin, 1993.

Reid I: Nationalism, Sport and Scotland's Culture, in, *Scottish Centre Research Papers in Sport, Leisure and Society*, vol 2, 1997.

Rowan P: *The Team That Jack Built*, Mainstream, Edinburgh, 1994.

Rouse P: The Politics of Culture and Sport in Ireland: A History of the GAA Ban on Foreign Games 1884–1971. Part One: 1884–1921, in, *The International Journal of the History of Sport*, vol 10, no 3, pp. 333–360, 1993.

Rowe D and Wood N (edts): Editorial of *Media, Culture and Society*, vol 18, no 4, 1996

Ryall T: *Kilkenny: The G.A.A. Story*, Published by The Kilkenny People, Kilkenny, 1984.

Schlesinger P: Media, the Political Order and National Identity, in *Media, Culture and Society*, vol 13, no 3, pp. 297–308, 1991.

Short C: *The Ulster G.A.A. Story*, Published by Comhairle Uladh CLG, printed by R&S Printers, Monaghan, 1984.

Sugden J and Bairner A: 'Northern Ireland; Sport in a Divided Society', in, Allison L, *The Politics Of Sport*, pp. 90–117, Manchester University Press, 1986.

Walker G and Gallagher T, (edts): *Sermons and Battle Hymns; Protestant Popular Culture in Modern Scotland*, Edinburgh University Press, 1990.

Whelan K: The Geography of Hurling, *History Ireland*, pp. 27–31, Vol 1, No 1, 1993.

Wilson B: Celtic, *A Century with Honour*, Willow Books, William Collins Publications, Glasgow, 1988.

Wilson D: Changed Utterly, *Fortnight*, pp. 5–6, October 1981.

Wilson J: *Politics and Leisure*, Unwin Hyman, Boston, 1988.

Newspapers referred to

Airdrie and Coatbridge Advertiser
Cork Free Press
Derry People
Donegal Democrat
Glasgow Observer and Catholic Herald
Irish News
The Fermanagh Herald
The Herald
The Irish Post
The Irish Weekly (Scotland)
The Kilkenny Journal
The Glasgow Examiner
The Glasgow Star and Examiner
Scottish Catholic Observer

Gaelic Publications referred to

Doire: A History of the G.A.A. in Derry, 1984.

G.A.A. Official Guide, 1994.

Gaelic Athletic Association: a century of service, 1984–1994, Published by the G.A.A., Dublin, 1984.

Hogan Stand.

John Mitchells Gaelic Football Club: The story of the G.A.A. in Liverpool. Centenary Year 1984–1984, Cumann Luthchleas Gael. Printed by Merchant Stationers Ltd, Liverpool, 1984.

The Sam Maguire Cup: Cumann Luthcleas Gael, Dublin, 1986.

Gaelsport G.A.A. Youth Annual: Gaelic Athletic Association, 1984.

Cead: A celebration of the London G.A.A., 1896–1996. Published by the London County Board in association with the Irish Post, Middlesex, 1996.

Also referred to

Cumann Luit Cleas Gaodeal, Ard Comairle Miontuirisci (Minutes of Central Council G.A.A.).

INDEX

Shows how the gaa has changed through the decades

chap 2 gives little mention to women's gaa

gaa was replaced by sinn fein

strong links between Ireland + Scot

gaa on up + down, a lot of effort went into its revival

as it was of ? imp to maj

change from hurling to gaelic pg 66.

Irish sport crept into univ this provided much opposition

for challenge games between scottish clubs

goes from one date to another - confusing

distinct between GAA in North + South.

made aware of exsistence of GAA in Scotland

only emphasised neg. effect of Irish in society not pos